KNOW-HOW

OF INVESTING IN CRYPTOCURRENCIES

Dan Vivek Nathan, MBA, MSc, B.A, FCIM (U.K)

First Edition

NEWMAN SPRINGS PUBLISHING
320 Broad Street
Red Bank, NJ 07701

First originally published by Newman Springs Publishing 2025

ISBN 979-8-89617-107-2 (Paperback)
ISBN 979-8-89617-109-6 (Hardcover)
ISBN 979-8-89617-108-9 (Digital)

Printed in the United States of America

CONTENTS

FOREWORD

It is my great pleasure to introduce this insightful book *Know-How of Investing in Cryptocurrencies* by Dan Vivek Nathan. He is a market analyst who has spent over four decades in marketing research and brings a much-needed perspective of cryptocurrency and investing know-how to the investment world. Investors will benefit not only from Nathan's vision of cryptocurrency investment but also his knowledge of Bitcoin and blockchain technology.

I was impressed by his deep understanding of the cryptocurrencies around the global cryptocurrency market and his ability to convey the road-map-guidance in investing in cryptocurrencies. This is my first recommendation for those looking for investments in cryptocurrencies that have driven the growth of the Bitcoin network and blockchain technology.

Whether you are a beginner in investing cryptocurrencies or stock market professional, you will find valuable insights that can help you navigate the current global cryptocurrency market. I highly recommend this book to anyone seeking to improve their cryptocurrency investment skills and achieve financial success. His guidance will undoubtedly serve as a valuable resource for years to come.

I hope you enjoy this book *Know-How of Investing in Cryptocurrencies* as much as I did and benefit from investing in cryptocurrencies.

A. Pritchard
Member of The Chartered Institute of Marketing, UK,
Member of The European Marketing Confederation, Belgium

CHAPTER 1

Knowledge of Cryptocurrency in the Digital Economy

Enterprising migration of the medium of exchange is a captivating field of inquiry. The evolution of how humans exchange value and facilitate trade—from bartering to commodity money to metallic money to paper money to current electronic money/digital money/currency. The current digital/virtual currencies are stored and transferred electronically via digital space. Virtual currency is a digital currency that is largely unregulated, issued and usually controlled by its developers, and used and accepted electronically among members of a specific virtual community. This form of electronic/virtual money has the benefit of being fast, secure, traceable, and accessible.

In essence, the history of money is the development over time of systems for the exchange, storage, and measurement of wealth. The concept of *money* has taken many different forms in human evolutionary history. We, as humans, worked with the barter system—trading goods such as livestock, seashells, silk, and spices, in exchange for land, food, and materials such as metals. Throughout human history, what people consider valuable has changed considerably. In essence, throughout human history, the concept of *money* has taken different forms—from trading goods and services to coins, bills [banknotes], checks, credit cards / debit cards, and *digital wallets* for *virtual money*/currency.

When it comes to livestock, the first form of currency, and the public frequently traded them for goods and seashells which were found in the Pacific and Indian Oceans, were traded as money. Then small pieces of metal as coins appeared, eventually bills [banknotes] represented the value of coins. The exchange of bills [banknotes] and coins transitioned to electronic transacting in the 1990s.

What Is Cryptocurrency?

A *cryptocurrency* is a digital currency designed to work as a medium of exchange via a computer network that is not reliant on any central authority, such as a government or bank, to uphold or maintain it. *Cryptocurrency* is a centralized system for verifying that the parties to a transaction have the money they claim to have, eliminating the need for traditional intermediaries such as banks, when funds are being transferred between two entities.

How Cryptocurrencies Work in a Nutshell?

When you want to use cryptocurrencies to purchase something, first, your cryptocurrency network and your cryptocurrency wallet automatically check your previous transactions to make sure you have enough cryptocurrencies to make that transaction. For this, you need your private and public keys.

The transactions are then encrypted, broadcast to the cryptocurrency's network, and queued up to be added to the public ledger.

Transactions are then recorded on the public ledger through *mining*. The sending and receiving addresses are wallet IDs or hash values that are not tied to the user identification, so they are anonymous.

For *Proof of Work* [PoW] cryptocurrencies, the miners have to solve a math puzzle to verify the transaction. *Proof of Stake* [PoS] cryptocurrencies attribute the *mining* power to the proportion of the coins held by the miners, instead of utilizing energy to solve math problems in order to resolve the wasted energy problem of *Proof of Work* [PoW].

Cryptocurrency plays a crucial role in the digital economy. For instance, cryptocurrencies furnish access to financial services for people who do not have to bank. In other words, two billion people worldwide do not have access to traditional banking systems. Cryptocurrencies enable these people to participate in the global economy.

The other reason is that unlike traditional systems controlled by central authorities, cryptocurrencies operate on decentralized networks. This, in turn, reduces the risk of a single point of failure and increases transparency and security.

The third reason is that cryptocurrencies can reduce the cost of transactions for cross-border payments. In brief, traditional banking systems often involve high fees and long processing times, whereas cryptocurrency transactions can be faster and cheaper.

The fourth reason is that the underlying blockchain technology of cryptocurrencies is driving innovation across various sectors—finance supply chain management and health care. The blockchain technology can improve efficiency, security, and transparency.

The fifth reason is that some cryptocurrencies such as bitcoin are seen as a hedge against inflation due to their limited supply. This can be applied in economies experiencing high inflation rates.

The sixth reason is that cryptocurrencies and blockchain technology are creating new economic opportunities, such as decentralized finance [DeFi], non-fungible tokens [NFT], and smart contracts. These innovations are eventually reshaping traditional business models and creating new markets.

Cryptocurrency has benefits. It reduces corruption, serving people without having bank accounts, giving people charge of their money, eliminating money printing by central banks, and no intermediaries such as banks.

Cryptocurrencies make transactions much easier and faster. Wallets play a crucial role in cryptocurrencies. The other important aspect of cryptocurrencies is getting a cryptocurrency exchange platform.

Investing in *cryptocurrency* makes sense. It takes control of your own money without relying on central banks. For instance, traditional investing stocks have some disadvantages:

1. Stocks face different types of risks—business and financial risk; purchasing power risk; market risk; global pandemic risk; government control and regulations; foreign competition; and the general state of the economy.
2. The stock selection process can be a pain in the neck. There are thousands of stocks to choose from. Predicting how the company will perform tomorrow can also be very difficult. The price today only reflects how the market participants feel about the current or future state of the company or that industry for that matter. By *investing* in the cryptocurrency market, you may be able to balance out some of the abovementioned risks.

Unfolding of Events of Fiat Currency and How It Becomes More Sophisticated

The outcome of the Bretton Woods meeting with delegates from forty-four countries on the 1st of July 1944 was an *International Gold Standard Agreement* where the US Dollar was downgraded to gold at $35 per troy ounce and other currencies were disrated to the dollar and could be redeemed for gold at the US Treasury. The IMF was established, as was the International Bank for Reconstruction and Development (IBRD) which would eventually become part of the World Bank. During that time, ordinary Americans were still banned from owning non-jewelry gold.

Prior to 1944, in the year 1931 Britain, most of the Commonwealth countries with the Bretton Woods marked a return to the gold standard. However, the Bretton Woods Agreement didn't work very well. Countries frequently devalued their currencies with respect to the US dollar and gold. In the year 1949, Britain devalued their Pound by about 30% from $4.30 to $2.80, and many other countries followed Britain. By 1971, the Bretton Woods Agreement broke down after the US stopped honoring the convertibility of US dollars to gold. Then there was a big drop in US gold reserves and an increase in foreign claims on US dollars.

How Fiat Currencies Come into Existence in the Financial System?

Quantitative Easing known as QE often comes up in fiat currencies. So the public describes this as *printing money*. QE is a metaphor for an authority, generally a *Central Bank,* increasing the amount of money in circulation in order to stimulate a flagging economy. So public worries that this additional money dilutes the value of existing money, and this makes the public worry about the sustainability of the *Fiat system*. In brief, Quantitative Easing is a form of monetary policy in which a central bank (like the US Federal Reserve) purchases predetermined amounts of government bonds or other financial assets in order to stimulate economic activity. In essence, Quantitative Easing is a form of monetary policy used by central bank to increase the domestic money supply and spur economic activity. Quantitative Easing creates new bank reserves, providing banks with more liquidity and encouraging lending and investment.

Quantitative Easing is often implemented where interest rates hover near zero and economic growth is stalled. To execute QE central banks, buy government bonds and other securities, injecting bank reserves into the economy. Increasing the supply of money lowers interest rates further and provides liquidity to the banking system, allowing banks to lend with easier terms. However, as money is increased in an economy, the risk of inflation looms.

Fiat Currency and Financial Technology (Fintech)

Fiat currency is not backed by a physical commodity such as gold or silver but, instead, backed by the government that issued it. Fiat currency derives its value from the decisions of the central bank, rather than through reserves of assets. In brief, the value of fiat currency is derived from the relationship between supply and demand and the stability of the issuing government, rather than the worth of a commodity backing it. In essence, fiat money generally does not have intrinsic value and does not have use value. It has value only because of the individuals who use it as a unit of accounting or in the case of currency, a medium of exchange.

Financial technology or Fintech is a term referring to the integration of technology into offerings by financial services companies in order to improve their use and delivery of service. For example, Artificial Intelligence (AI), blockchain, cloud computing, big data, etc. are considered the key areas of Fintech. In industry, Fintech has been used to automate investments, insurance, trading, banking services, and risk management. Fintech can apply to any innovation in how people transact businesses, from the invention of digital money to double-entry bookkeeping.

The crucial aspect of the use of artificial intelligence tools to automate the application, screening, and approval processes involved in the provision of credit, insurance, and other financial products. These factors reduce the costs of entry for new companies/businesses and products in addition to erasing some of the advantages of established companies/businesses such as experienced employees, expertise, deep pockets, and name recognition.

Advanced technologies help overcome one of the major barriers to rapid change from the user perspective—network effects, which in this context refers to the convenience of adopting a payment method or service that is already in widespread use, rather than switching to a new alternative. Another Fintech innovation is the advent of mobile/smartphone-based applications designed to facilitate the use of money and banking.

Artificial Intelligence (AI) algorithms can furnish insight into customer spending habits, allowing financial institutions to better understand their clients. Chatbots are Artificial Intelligence–driven tools that banks are starting to utilize to help with customer service. Big data can predict client investments and market changes in order to create new strategies and portfolios, analyze customer spending habits, improve fraud detection, and create marketing strategies. The decentralized nature of blockchain can eliminate the need for a third party to execute transactions. Fintech also includes the development and use of cryptocurrencies such as Bitcoin.

In essence, Fintech is utilized to help companies, business owners, and consumers better manage their financial operations, processes, and lives. Fintech is composed of specialized software and algorithms that are used on computers and smartphones. Examples of Fintech applications include payment apps, peer-to-peer lending apps, investment apps, crypto apps, etc.

How Does Quantitative Easing Work?

The *Central Bank* buys assets such as bonds, funds from the private commercial sector, commercial banks, asset managers, and hedge funds in the secondary market. The bonds that have already been issued and now traded by financial market participants.

Central banks form an image of the private sector as having a balance of two things—*money* and *nonmoney* and other financial assets. Central banks control those balances by buying financial assets from the private sector to add money or by selling financial assets to the private sector to remove money. But when it comes to bonds, they are generally safe assets. Their value is affected by interest rates—the central bank has some control over it. Central banks buy bonds from certain clearing banks. Central banks start the QE journey by buying government bonds—US Treasury, etc.

CHAPTER 2

Bitcoin—How It Works?

Let us see what *Bitcoin* is. It is the most prominent member of a *new class of electronic money* known as *cryptocurrency*, which exists *only* in the *digital world*. Cryptocurrency has underlying digital technology in the blockchain, which is a series of blocks that when combined, act as a permanent, unalterable ledger, detailing the *history* of transactions in a *cryptocurrency*. Blockchain plays an important role in investing in cryptocurrency.

Bitcoin (BTC) runs on a blockchain a digital ledger logging transaction distributed across a network of numerous computers. The additions to the digitally distributed ledgers have to be verified—by proof of work. Bitcoin is the most prominent member of the class of electronic money known as *cryptocurrency*, which exists only in the digital space. It is often compared to a *Digital Ledger Book*. The *computer code* upon which it is based keeps everyone honest by making account balances/transactions, all of which are electronic and are fully visible as public digital ledgers maintained on the Internet. However, a few cryptographic concepts are among the building *blocks*/records for Bitcoin. These have to do with maintaining the confidentiality of transacting parties and the integrity of the public digital ledgers. Also, the identities of the people who use *Bitcoin*, on the other hand, remain hidden.

Digital Public and Private Keys Involve in Bitcoin

These are individual user *identities*. The public digital keys are distributed widely without compromising security. One must know both the username and password to operate the account. These digital keys constitute the essential elements and anonymous digital payment systems.

Bitcoin is the very first digital asset of value that can be transferred over the Internet without any specific third party having to approve the transaction. It is an asset that is transferred from one individual owner to another individual than moving through a series of third party—debits or credits—via one or more banks.

Bitcoins are digital assets or coins whose ownership is recorded on an electronic ledger that is updated simultaneously on several thousands of computers around the globe that connect and circulate with each other. This electronic ledger is known as Bitcoin's *blockchain*. Transactions that record the transfer of ownership of those coins are created and validated according to a protocol, a list of rules that define how things work, and which therefore update to the electronic ledger.

The protocol is implemented by a software application that participants run on their computers. The computers running the software applications are known as *nodes* of the network. A node is a computer that connects to a cryptocurrency network. A *node* is an electronic device doing the *bookkeeping* job in the *blockchain* making the whole decentralized thing possible. The *node* can be a computer, a cell phone, or even a printer, as long as it's connected to the Internet and has access to the *blockchain* network. Each *node* independently validated all pending transactions wherever they arose and updated its own record of the electronic ledger with validated *blocks*/records of confirmed transactions. Specialist *nodes* called miners, bundle together valid transactions into *blocks*/records and distribute those *blocks*/records to *nodes* across the network. Any individual can purchase bitcoins, own them, and send them to others. However, every Bitcoin transaction is recorded and shared publicly in plain text on Bitcoin's blockchain.

Any individual can create Bitcoins for themselves, and this is known as block creating process—*mining*. Much of the mining of Bitcoin is carried out by specialized devices known as ASIC [Application Specific Integrated Circuits]. ASICs are built machines containing computer chips designed with a single specific purpose.

Bitcoin and Other Coins

Bitcoin is the first type of cryptocurrency in the financial world. It is widely used and accepted around the globe. Bitcoin is a decentralized digital currency that utilizes *peer-to-peer* technology and is referred to as *blockchain*. This is to *verify transactions*. It runs on a high-powered *computer network* that stores its *codes* and *blockchain*, making it a *secure system* that is difficult for hackers to attack.

We find there are several thousands of cryptocurrencies in the global landscape. All types of cryptocurrencies share certain characteristics. They are all forms of *digital currencies* that allow for electronic transactions. However, there are some key differences among them:

Litecoin: This is a decentralized digital currency that operates on an open-source global payment not controlled by a central authority such as a bank or government. It offers a faster transaction time than *Bitcoin*.

Ripple [XRP]: It is a global payment *network* that serves major banks and financial institutions, including *Bank of America* and *Royal Bank of Canada*. Ripple's main focus is as a payment settlement asset exchange and remittances system, similar to the *swift* system for international money and security transfers used by banks and financial intermediaries dealing across currencies.

Solana [SOL]: Developed to help power *Decentralized Finance* [DeFi] uses, decentralized applications and *smart contracts*. It runs on unique hybrid proof-of-stakes and proof-of-history mechanisms to process transactions quickly and securely. This is a solid competitor to *Ethereum* with faster transaction speeds and lower fees. This is a proof-of-stake *blockchain*. This is one of the most popular cryptocurrencies trading today. It is a decentralized and open-source *blockchain* designed to be scalable, fast, and secure. It can process a significantly higher number of transactions than other popular *blockchain* platforms like *Ethereum* and *Bitcoin*.

Dogecoin [DOGE]: It is a Bitcoin-based digital cryptocurrency. This is the most famous called *meme coin*. There is no limit on the number of *Dogecoins* that can be created. It is a *peer-to-peer*, open-source cryptocurrency. Users can purchase and sell *Dogecoin* in digital currency exchange.

Chainlink [LINK]: This a cryptocurrency based upon a *decentralized Oracle network*, which allows it to connect data from the outside world to any *blockchain*. This structure gives developers more opportunities to build flexible and secure applications.

Cardano [ADA]: It works like *Ethereum* to enable *smart contracts* and *decentralized* applications. This is a *blockchain* that offers *decentralized* financial products, similar to *Ethereum* but operates on a proof-of-stakes *blockchain*. This lets people mine or validate block transactions according to how many coins they have. It is different from most *blockchains*. You can create tokens on Cardano without *smart contracts*.

Stellar [XLM]: This open *blockchain technology* can be utilized by anyone but was primarily designed to support large transactions between financial institutions. In essence, it is an open-source, *decentralized* protocol for digital currency to fiat money low-cost transfers which allows cross-border transactions between any pair of currencies. The platform's source code is hosted on GitHub.

Polkadot [DOT]: This is a proof-of-stake cryptocurrency designed to secure users' identities by connecting *blockchains* and networks. Polkadot's network is capable of interacting with other *blockchain* networks. It allows developers to create *decentralized* applications on its platform.

Binance [BNB]: This cryptocurrency serves as a payment method for trading fees associated with the *Binance Exchange* where users can trade cryptocurrencies—one of the largest *crypto exchanges*. Binance can be used for trading, payment processing, and booking travel arrangements. It can also be traded and exchanged for other forms of cryptocurrency—*Ethereum* or *Bitcoin*.

Coinbase [COIN]: It is a publicly traded company that operates a cryptocurrency *exchange platform*. Coinbase is a distributed company. All employees operate via remote work. It offers products for both retail and institutional cryptocurrency investors, as well as other related cryptocurrency products.

Tether [USDT]: Tether's value is connected to regular fiat currencies to keep its price more stable than its competitors. In other words, it is backed by fiat currencies [US Dollars and EU Dollars]. This type of arrangement is known as *Stablecoin*.

Monero [XMR]: It offers users more privacy than other cryptocurrencies. It uses a special technique called ring signatures which hide the identities of the sender and receiver of every transaction as well as the amount.

Shiba Inu [SHIB]: This is another *meme coin*. This is an *Ethereum*-based *Altcoin* other than *Bitcoin*. This is the project's foundational currency.

Dash [DASH]: This is an open-source cryptocurrency, which means it is collaboratively produced, freely shared, and published transparently. It supports daily transactions and can be used as cash or credit or via PayPal.

ZCash [ZEC]: It uses cryptography and coding to provide enhanced privacy to users. Users can choose whether or not to anonymize the information associated with their transactions.

Waves [WAVES]: This is a *blockchain* designed to help users create and launch custom crypto tokens. The platform is designed to make it easier to develop new types of tokens without needing to understand the complicated programming language.

Neo [NEO]: It is much more environmentally friendly. It does not charge transaction fees.

Lisk [LSK]: This is an open-source *blockchain* application platform. The utility token affiliated with *Lisk* is *Lisk*, which can be used to pay for transaction fees on the *Lisk blockchain*.

Tron [TRX]: This is a *blockchain*-based *decentralized* platform. It aims to eliminate the middleman between content creators and content consumers by allowing consumers to directly pay creators to access their content. This is a *blockchain* designed to run *smart contacts* and other *Decentralized Finance* [DeFi] applications.

Uniswap [UNI]: This is a *decentralized* exchange that runs on the *Ethereum blockchain*. It allows trades in other cryptocurrencies and offers its own native tokens, which give holders the right to change the protocols governing the exchange.

Stablecoin: Stablecoin is a cryptocurrency that aims to maintain price stability by pegging its monetary value to a given fiat currency, typically on a one-to-one basis. Stablecoins offer a less risky alternative to store money on the *blockchain* and facilitate payments between individuals and institutions alike. They are accessible worldwide to anyone with an Internet connection and are functional 24-7. They are fast and inexpensive to use. Through the use of *smart contracts*, transactions can be automatically executed within specific parameters. It can be used for trading, borrowing, and lending, earning yield, as an alternative to banking for sending remittances, as stores of value, etc.

Examples of Fiat-Based *Stable Coins*:

1. USDC [*Coinbase*]
2. *Tether*
3. GUSD[*Gemini*]
4. BUSD[*Binance*]

FEATURES OF BITCOIN:
There are some main features of Bitcoin:

1. Bitcoin's trading symbol is BTC.
2. Bitcoin is minable.
3. Coin creation occurs through proof-of-work [PoW].
4. Transaction time is between thirty minutes and twenty-four hours.
5. Transactions are not fully anonymous.
6. Bitcoin is decentralized.
7. Mining Bitcoin requires a lot of energy.

Bitcoin is a decentralized digital *cryptocurrency*. Bitcoin [BTC] operates without a central authority such as a bank or government.

How Bitcoin works: First, select a Bitcoin trade exchange platform to get a Bitcoin wallet to use Bitcoin. This Bitcoin wallet generates a unique address for sending/receiving BTC. Each BTC wallet has a secret code [which is a private key] that allows a person to access and manage his/her BTC.

When a person sends a BTC, the BTC wallet uses the private key/secret code to sign the transaction, proving that he/she owns the BTC being transferred. This transaction is then broadcast to the network and included in the blockchain once verified.

Mining is the process of verifying and adding transactions to the blockchain. The mining process involves maintaining the blockchain through computer processing power. Miners group and broadcast new transactions into blocks, which are then verified by the network. Each block must contain proof of work [PoW] to be accepted.

Invest Bitcoin in a Nutshell

First, select a BTC exchange platform. In other words, BTC investor has to find an exchange platform such as Kraken as a stock brokerage. Then, get a BTC wallet. BTC is stored in a wallet, either a hot wallet or in a cold wallet. For example, hot wallet includes Electrum software which enables the storage of BTC on a computer. Cold wallet, which is hardware, for example, Trezor that stores coins.

Then, link/connect to your bank account. This enables you to buy BTC.

Now, it is time to buy BTC. Your exchange platform will have everything you need to buy.

Manage your BTC investments. Your exchange platform will furnish you with everything you need to buy and sell BTC.

Some of the most active areas of fintech innovation include the following:

1. Cryptocurrency – Bitcoin, Ethereum, Digital Tokens (non-fungible tokens) and digital cash. These rely upon blockchain technology, which is distributed ledger technology (DLT) that maintains records on a network of computers (nodes) but has no central ledger. Blockchain allows for *smart contracts* that utilize code to automatically execute contracts between parties such as buyers and sellers.

2. Open banking
3. Simplify and streamline the insurance industry
4. Help financial services firms meet industry compliance rules.
5. Utilize algorithms to automate investment advice to lower its cost and increase accessibility.
6. Underbanked services that seek to serve disadvantaged or low-income individuals.
7. Cybersecurity
8. Artificial Intelligence (AI) Chatbots.

The main question is, Will *Fiat money* survive in the years to come?

Some believe that the public as a whole has some challenges in the *global digital economy* in the form of *digital currency—cryptocurrencies.*

Difference between Fiat Currency and Virtual Currency

Fiat Currency is money that is issued by the decree of a government. The value of a fiat currency is based on the strength of the issuing country's economy. For instance, the Dollar is considered one of the global economy's most valuable currencies since the United States of America is one of the world's largest and strongest economies. The idea of value as it relates to currency shifted again in the twenty-first century with the rise of *digital currencies* such as *Bitcoin* and others. In essence, hard currency rarely needs to change hands, and the reliance on digital transactions has helped to give rise to a new way to pay: *cryptocurrency.*

The first such form, *Bitcoin,* replaced the *central authority* of a bank with peer-to-peer *computer technology.* Today, we see tremendous growth in several cryptocurrencies. *Bitcoin* is like a digital ledger book. In other words, the computer code upon which it is based keeps everyone honest by making account balances and transactions public. The identities of the people who use *Bitcoin,* on the other hand, remain hidden.

CHAPTER 3

Knowledge of Mining

Not all cryptocurrencies can be mined. Bitcoin and some other coins [for example, Ripple (XRP) can be mined. *Mining* consumes an enormous amount of *energy* in the process of mining. *Power* usage is one of the issues with *blockchain.*

Before getting started with *mining*, you should set yourself up with a few things. When you have got everything up and running, *mining* becomes rather easy because everything happens automatically. The only thing left to do is pay your electric bills at the end of each month.

1. Get a cryptocurrency wallet.
2. Make sure you have a strong Internet connection.
3. Set up your high-end computer in a cool location.
4. Select the hardware to use based on the cryptocurrency you want to *mine.*
5. If you want to mine solo, download the whole cryptocurrency's *blockchain.*
6. Get a *mining software* package.
7. Join a *mining* pool.
8. Make sure your expenses do not exceed your rewards.

Mining is the process of verifying and adding *transactions* to the *blockchain*. The mining process involves maintaining the blockchain through computing processing power. In other words, cryptocurrency miners solve cryptographic puzzles via *software* to add transactions to the ledger [the *blockchain* in the hope of getting coins as a reward. Miners group a broadcast new transaction into blocks, which are then verified by the networks. Each block must contain proof of work [PoW] to be accepted. If you are a miner and want to enter your *block* and transactions into the *blockchain*, you have to provide an answer or *proof* to a specific challenge, this process is called proof-of-work [PoW].

There is an alternative called proof-of-stake [PoS]. The proof-of-stake system requires you to show ownership of a certain amount of money or stake. In other words, the more cryptocurrency you own, the more mining power you have.

Then, there is proof of authority [PoA]. This is about the value of identity and reputation. For instance, Microsoft Azure is using PoA in its Ethereum-powered cloud computing system, offering solutions.

Mining Cryptocurrency

It is the process of procreating *new coins* and verifying *new transactions*. This process involves wide decentralized computer networks around the globe that verify and secure B*lockchain-virtual ledgers* that document transactions of cryptocurrencies.

Mining in cryptocurrency is performed utilizing sophisticated hardware that solves complex computational mathematical problems. For example, hardware such as ASICs, which stands for Application-Specific Integrated Circuits has been customized to optimize cryptocurrencies like Bitcoin and Bitcoin Cash. Bitcoin mining is the process of authenticating the information in a *blockchain's* block by procreating a cryptographic solution that matches specific criteria. However, when a correct solution is reached, a *reward* in the form of *Bitcoin* and fees for the work done are given to the miners who reached the solution first.

How Mining in Cryptocurrency Works

Cryptocurrency miners solve cryptographic puzzles through *software* to add transactions to the *ledger*—the *blockchain* in the hope of getting coins as a reward. This is known as *mining*. This is because of the fact that this process helps extract *new cryptocurrencies* from the system.

Anyone can join this group. But your computer needs to guess a random number that solves an equation that the *blockchain* system generates.

Your computer has to calculate many 64-character strings or 256-bit hashes and check with the challenge equation to see whether the answer is right. That is why it is so vital that you have a powerful computer. The more powerful your computer is, the more guesses it can make in a second, increasing your chances of winning. If you manage to guess right, you earn Bitcoins and get to write the next page of Bitcoin transactions on the *blockchain*. The fact of the matter is *mining* is based on a form of guessing, for each *block* a different miner guesses the number and is granted the right to update the *blockchain*. The biggest computer power will be the first to solve the challenge equation and win.

If you want to enter your *block* and transactions into the *blockchain*, you need to provide the answer—*proof-of-work* [PoW] to a specific challenge. One of the main challenges is that it consumes enormous computing power and electricity for producing random guesses.

So new cryptocurrencies have an alternative known as *proof of stake* [PoS]. It requires you to show ownership of a certain amount of money or stake. The more cryptocurrencies you own, the more *mining* power you have. This approach eliminates the need for an expensive process. The calculations are pretty simple to prove, you own a certain percentage of the total amount of cryptocurrencies available. The *proof of stake* offers no *block* rewards, so the miners get transaction fees. *proof of stake* can be several thousand times more cost-effective than *proof of work* [PoW].

There is another *proof of stake* known as *delegated proof of stake* [DPoS]. For each new *block*, the network chooses a limited number of delegates. This number is anywhere between twenty and a hundred. There is a chance that a network could become more centralized than traditional *blockchain* mechanisms.

There is *proof of authority* [PoA] which is about the value of identity and reputation. The validation on a PoA *blockchain* does not stake coins. Instead, they stake their reputation. That means PoAs are secured by selected nodes. This mechanism is typically used by private networks and companies who want to maintain their privacy while reaping the benefits of *blockchain* without the need for a native currency or the need for *mining*. In brief, PoA wastes a whole lot less energy to operate. For example, supply chain networks and Microsoft Azure where PoA is being implemented. Microsoft Azure is using PoA in its Ethereum-powered cloud computing system. PoA is centralized. It is primarily an attempt to improve the efficiency of traditional centralized systems.

There is another mechanism. It is known as *proof of history* [PoH]. PoH is kike a clock that stamps transactions with a hash. This shows when the transaction happened and makes it valid. The networks do not need to worry about verifying the time claims of nodes. They can rely on the system to do this. This makes it easier for nodes to process *blocks* and put them in the ledger.

Anyone can start *cryptocurrency mining*.

1. First, select a cryptocurrency that you want to do mining. For instance, *Bitcoin* [BTC}, *Ethereum* [ETH], etc. Each has hardware requirements.
2. Then, try to get the exact hardware. For example, *Bitcoin* has *apps* with an integrated circuit known as ASIC. Other hardware includes a Graphic Processing Unit [GPU].
3. Now, try to set up a *wallet* to store the cryptocurrency you mine. This includes hardware wallet, software wallet, and online wallet.
4. Now, download mining software. For example, Awesome Miner, EasyMiner, CGMiner, BFG Miner, and NiceHash

[Awesome Miner's interface manages all your mining activity in one program. It runs on Windows, Linux, and cloud-based web on any other browser; EasyMiner is one of the easiest and fastest mining software to set up; CGminer is one of the oldest and most popular examples of Bitcoin mining software. It supports ASICs and GPUs.]

5. Try to join a mining pool to combine your computerized power with others. This will increase your chances of earning *rewards*.
6. Then, configure your miner. This involves entering the mining pool address and your wallet address.
7. Once everything is set up, *start* mining. Try to monitor your hardware's performance. Ensure hardware is cooled enough and maintained.
8. Since *mining* is energy-intensive, electricity and hardware maintenance are needed. Try to *calculate* whether it is *profitable*.

Bitcoin and Mining

Bitcoin mining is a complex computational and technological process of validating Bitcoin transactions over the Bitcoin network. It is like a process of validating a block/record on the chain network and getting paid in bitcoins. Mining is the process of adding transaction records to Bitcoins' public ledger of past transactions.

There are many ways to earn bitcoins. Mining for bitcoins is how bitcoin participates in the network. Anyone gets started earning *Bitcoins*. Mining for Bitcoins is usually handled by special mining hardware. This mining hardware is expensive as well as specialized. It also needs *Bitcoin mining software* to connect to the blockchain and the mining pool. The mining pool is a collection of many miners jointly working together and then splitting the rewards of their efforts.

Let us see the different mining Bitcoin software:

1. CGminer. It is open-source and is available for Windows, Linux, and OS: www.github.com/ckolivas/cgminer
2. Bitcoin-QT: https://bitcoin.org/en/download
3. Multiminerapp: Download it at www.multiminerapp.com

What Is a Digital Wallet?

A cryptocurrency wallet is a software program that helps you manage your digital money. In terms of *virtual money*/currency, digital transactions are stored. It can be a piece of paper, a hardware device that plugs into your computer, an app on your computer, or even on your mobile device. These *digital wallets* allow users to send and receive *digital currency*, by providing an *internet address* to which tokens can be sent. In other words, a *digital wallet* is a method of storing the public and private keys needed to access your *digital currency*.

Let us see how to maintain a *digital wallet*:

A digital currency needs a *digital wallet*. Crypto wallets hold public and private encryption keys. These key wallets are used for buying or selling digital currency. There are two categories of digital wallets:

1. A hot wallet is connected to the Internet. Any app-based wallet or a wallet that is accessed via a computer's browser is known as a hot wallet. These hot wallets make accessing crypto easier.
2. A cold wallet is not directly connected to the Internet. These are small portable devices similar to USB drives.

- Wallet address – A number that functions something like a traditional bank.

The Steps to Buy Cryptocurrencies

1. Choose the place to buy – You can choose from cryptocurrency exchanges operating in your area/country/cryptocurrency brokers or even ATMs.
2. Select your method of payment – Most exchanges allow you to purchase cryptocurrency using the fiat currency of your country like the US dollar. One of the easiest methods to buy is connecting your bank account or other payment options to the exchange. Before being able to pay, most exchanges require personal identification methods, including pictures of your driver's license or social security card. Sometimes you need to pay a fee for the transactions. The fees vary depending on your method of payment and the exchange policy.
3. Search for the cryptocurrency you have decided to invest in. Discover different types of cryptocurrencies and how to select the ones that are most suitable to your risk tolerance.
4. Select the price and the amount of cryptocurrency you would like to invest in. Most cryptocurrency exchanges and brokers allow you to set something called a *buy limit order* to purchase your cryptocurrency assets at your optimal price. By conducting technical analysis and combining that with your risk tolerance you may decide to either purchase your favorite cryptocurrency asset at the current market price or set a buy limit order to purchase at future potentially lower prices.

Let us see the different *exchanges*:

1. Digital Currency Exchange [DCE]. It is a web service that can help people exchange their cash into cryptocurrencies and vice versa. Most exchanges are more focused on providing services to help you exchange a cryptocurrency such as Bitcoin into other digital currencies like Ethereum, Dogecoin, etc. Most exchanges operate online.

The following are the cryptocurrency exchanges:

1. Centralized cryptocurrency exchange [CEX] – CEXs are similar to traditional stock exchanges. *Centralize* means to trust somebody else to handle your money. The buyers and sellers come together, and the exchange plays the role of an intermediary. These exchanges typically charge a commission to facilitate the transactions made between the buyers and the sellers.

How a centralized exchange works:

(a) Give your money to the exchange.
(b) The exchange holds it for you like a bank or a trusted intermediary.
(c) You can see the prices of the available cryptocurrencies on the exchange.
(d) Depending on the exchange, you can trade your fiat currency such as the US dollar for a cryptocurrency such as Bitcoin. With most exchanges, you find better luck exchanging two cryptocurrencies for one another.
(e) You place your order.
(f) The exchange finds a seller to match your buy order. If you are selling the exchange finds you a buyer.

Most centralized cryptocurrency exchanges have cryptocurrency pairings. It involves exchanging one cryptocurrency such as Bitcoin for another cryptocurrency such as Ethereum.

Centralized cryptocurrency exchanges are user-friendly and offer a support system to beginner investors.

The most popular centralized cryptocurrency exchanges that offer fiat/cryptocurrency pairings include the following:

1. *Binance* – It offers an online cryptocurrency wallet for traders to store their assets. It also supports interest-earning ser-

vices. There are over 1000 cryptocurrencies worldwide. It is one of the cheapest/inexpensive exchange platforms to use transaction fees are pretty low.

2. *Coinbase* – Coinbase exchange is one of the beginner-friendly cryptocurrency platforms and offers basic transactions, a digital wallet, and easy withdrawals. For more complicated investment methods, they also have a pro platform. Coinbase supports over 200 cryptocurrencies and is insured. You can use the US dollar (USD), the Euro (EUR), the Australian dollar (AUD), and the British pound (GBP) to fund your account and to buy and sell cryptocurrencies. It also offers a Visa debit card that is accepted worldwide.
3. *Gemini* – The exchange is focused on security and ease of use and supports over 200 cryptocurrencies.
4. Decentralized cryptocurrency exchanges [DEX] – This is an exchange that does not rely on an intermediary to hold your funds. It is a marketplace where buyers and sellers come together and process the transactions directly between one another. DEXs facilitate peer-to-peer trades. You would be able to make the deals through things like *smart contracts* [Smart contracts are self-executing contracts where the terms of the agreement between buyer and seller are directly written into lines of code.]

Examples of Decentralized exchanges:

1. Curve – It is a popular automated maker [AMM] platform. It offers a very efficient way to exchange tokens. It has low fees. The reason for this is that only it works with liquidity pools made up of assets that have similar behavior patterns.
2. *Dodo* – It uses Ethereum and Binance Smart Chain. It aims to make Decentralized Finance [DeFi] liquidity more accessible. It uses its own proactive market-maker algorithm.
3. PancakeSwap – It is a place where people can trade the NB Chain ecosystem and one of the top DEXs by mar-

ket share. It employs an automated market maker (AMM) model, allowing users to trade against a liquidity pool.

4. Uniswap – With Uniswap, you can easily trade cryptocurrency tokens without having to create an account. You can earn interest in your cryptocurrency through Uniswap's liquidity pools. Uniswap does not permit buying or selling cryptocurrency. You also cannot buy cryptocurrency using regular money on this exchange. You can only use cryptocurrency that you already have in a digital wallet.
5. Hybrid cryptocurrency exchanges – The hybrid cryptocurrency exchanges aim to merge benefits from both DEXs and CEXs to give consumers the best of both worlds.
6. Decentralized cryptocurrency exchange [DEX] – DEXs aim to stay true to the pure philosophy behind the cryptocurrency industry.
7. Hybrid cryptocurrency exchange – These are known to be the next-generation cryptocurrency trading marketplace. They combine the best CEXs and DEXs.

Anyone can purchase a *cryptocurrency*:

1. Before you purchase your first cryptocurrency coin, you will have to have a place to keep it in your cryptocurrency *wallet*. Most exchanges offer a default wallet that you can use. However, you can have a secure wallet known as a cold wallet.
2. Try to select an exchange or trading platform.
3. Once you have selected an exchange, create an account and verify your identity – personal information, copy of your driver's license, and proof of your address.
4. You must make a decision on how much you want to invest.
5. Once you have selected an exchange, set up an account, and decided how much you want to spend, you are ready to make your purchase.

But if you don't want to go through an exchange, or you want to convert cash to coins, another option is Bitcoin ATM. Insert cash, and the ATM will give you a QR code you can use to send the coins directly to your digital wallet.

Let us look at cryptocurrency exchange platforms:

Cryptocurrency exchanges are online platforms that enable users to *buy*, *sell*, and *trade* various cryptocurrencies. Many of these exchange platforms allow anyone to purchase cryptocurrencies with US dollars. From there, anyone can trade one type of cryptocurrency coin for another.

There are two types of cryptocurrency exchange platforms, namely, *centralized* and *decentralized.*

Centralized exchange platforms are simple to use. Here transactions are facilitated through a third party. For example, Binance or Coinbase. To use a centralized exchange platform, he or she first registers and proof of identification, this grants access to certain privileges that a decentralized exchange platform does not offer.

Decentralized exchange platforms have a steeper learning curve. Transactions on decentralized exchange platforms are made directly between traders. For example, on the decentralized platforms trades are conducted across user-owned distributed ledgers. This makes the system much more difficult to hack.

When it comes to a *public key*, it is similar to a username—shareable string numbers and letters that allow users to send and receive *digital currency*. A *Private key* is like a password, a private number that allows an owner to access their *digital currency*.

Let's look at the advantages and disadvantages of cryptocurrency on a global scale:

Advantages:

1. Cryptocurrency can directly impact and change important financial in global trade which can be made faster

and more affordable through cryptocurrency *transactions.* Cryptocurrency also can make global transfers more effectively and efficiently feeless, whilst online banking has struggled to keep these fees under one percent.

2. Blockchain *transactions* are the fastest type of financial transfer and are also one of the most *secure* due to every transaction being recorded.
3. Utilizing blockchain technology for transfers, as everything remains anonymous. Everyone can see the *transactions* happening and access the records at any time, but identities remain unknown. In essence, it furnishes a sense of privacy and security that many have longed for with their *transactions.*
4. There are numerous advantages to having *cryptocurrency.* In other words, the developers/designers of the network of Bitcoin systems have built properties into their systems that have made cryptocurrency a competitive alternative *financial system*, for example, Electronic Payment Systems such as PayPal, credit cards, and banks.
5. They have *low* transaction costs, unlike other systems such as Electronic Payment Systems—PayPal where transfer of money with banks tends to have expensive fees. In essence, it costs less to transfer money from one individual to another individual. Businesses also don't have to account for added expenses which eventually translate into lower prices for the consumers/customers. Moreover, immigrants who left their home country to find work and want to send remittances back to their families.
6. In the twenty-first century, banks and financial institutions around the globe don't serve poor, rural areas, particularly smaller countries. However, *cryptocurrency* works to combat poverty and oppression around the world. In other words, *free* and *open* access to basic financial services could easily help those who are impoverished and oppressed. Bitcoin furnishes any individual with Internet access with robust financial services.

7. Cryptocurrency has its speed, its facilitation of the digital nature of micro-payments, and its low transaction costs. This leads to innovating new marketing and business models, financial opportunities, and online business strategies.
8. Cryptocurrency is also untaxable as no central body owns it. In brief, people are in control of the finances of cryptocurrency, which means further savings for businesses and companies. This can deeply benefit larger businesses, which means funds can be spent on improving the businesses or extending growth instead of paying higher business taxes.
9. Developers/designers of open-source *cryptocurrency* can extend functionalities by writing APIs and application-specific code to interact with networks of *cryptocurrency*.
10. Transactions of *cryptocurrency* process quicker than checks and transfer of bank-facilitated money transfers. These transactions are recorded in the *cryptocurrency*'s public ledger. In other words, the transactions are recorded in the permanent transaction BLOCKCHAIN.
11. The ***private key*** [cryptographic ***password***] is the only way money can be accessed. In essence, no bank, company, or central government can *freeze* your *assets*.

Disadvantages:

1. *Cryptocurrency* fluctuates in value.
2. There are digital security breaches.
3. There are open opportunities in Bitcoin for criminals to partake in illegal activities such as money laundering, funding for terrorists, and the exchange of illegal goods and services.

Use of Cryptocurrency for Consumers/ Customers around the Globe

One of the objectives of cryptocurrency is to expand access to financial service tools to many people who are barred from entering the traditional banking system. It encourages self-sovereignty, the ability for individuals to maintain control over their data, be it identity information or their money. As cryptocurrencies gain more popularity, more and more companies are accepting them as a form of payment.

There are several companies such as *Microsoft*, *T-Mobile, PayPal, Starbucks, Home Depot, Expedia, Whole Foods, Subway, Pizza Hut,* etc. accept cryptocurrency as payment or use it for transactions. They partner with payment processors such as GoCoin, Coinbase, and BitPay to accept cryptocurrencies—Bitcoin, Ethereum, Dogecoin, Cardano, etc. Around 50% of companies around the world accept cryptocurrencies as a form of payment. Ninety percent of retailers accept cryptocurrency as a form of payment.

CHAPTER 4

Blockchain-—How It Works?

In layman's terms, a blockchain is an encrypted network used to store, distribute, and generate information. The key to a blockchain lies in the way it connects the information on it. In other words, a blockchain is like a *database* that runs on a network of computers. A series of *blocks*/records that, when combined, act as a permanent, unalterable *ledger*, detailing the history of *transactions* in *cryptocurrency*. It is a *database* shared across many different computers. In brief, the blockchain started life as a *distributed ledger* used to authenticate a *cryptocurrency*'s transaction history. Now, it is being used as the basis for all sorts of secure transactions, from secure information exchange to smart contracts, art ownership, and more.

Before going further, it is vital to note that not every blockchain is made the same. While there are a number of variable features, two of the most important are the *openness* of the platform (public or private) and the level of permissions required to add information to the blockchain (permissioned or permissionless). Public blockchains (like Bitcoin) are open for anyone to read and view, while private blockchains can only be viewed by a chosen group of people. Similarly, permissioned blockchains permit just a select group of users to write/generate transactions for the ledger to record and commit very few new blocks for addition to the chain. In contrast, permissionless blockchains allow anyone to contribute and add data to the ledger.

In brief, A blockchain is a shared ledger of transactions between parties in a network, not controlled by a single central authority. You can think of a ledger like a record book. It records and stores all transactions between users in chronological order. Instead of one authority controlling this ledger (like a bank), an identical copy of the ledger is held by all users on the network, called *nodes* (computers).

In a blockchain, consecutive, time-stamped transactions are grouped into segments known as *blocks*/records. Each *block*/record is sealed with complex encryption. The next *block*/record links to the previous *block*/record, and the chain grows, single *block* by single *block*/record, as more *transactions* occur. All the *blocks*/records on a blockchain are related to one another. Each *block*/record is protected with complex encryption. As *blocks*/records get linked, they create a permanent *transaction* history visible to the entire network. Since they are also decentralized, there is no intermediary overseeing the transaction database.

No single user can override or alter the blockchain's history. That makes blockchain an extremely secure system. Blockchains are an excellent tool for launching a whole new era of *financial innovation*. They eliminate the need for centralized authority to oversee *transactions*, blockchains have the potential to disrupt many parts of the *financial services* industry, including banks, brokers, and lenders. Furthermore, blockchain technology can be useful for providing banking-type services to people who have historically avoided doing business with banking institutions.

The blockchain requires the participation of many different users dedicating computing power to growing and maintaining the blockchain. A blockchain incentivizes this participation by rewarding those users who grow the blockchain with native *cryptocurrency*, a process known as *mining*.

ILLUSTRATIVE FLOWCHART OF BLOCKCHAIN

In brief, a Blockchain is a *distributed ledger* with a growing list of *blocks*/records that are securely linked together through *cryptographic hashes*. For the purposes of a cryptocurrency, a *hash* serves as a digital fingerprint of a transaction. Each transaction has a unique *hash*. Only that specific transaction with all the relevant information coded in exactly the same fashion as before, will reproduce that *hash*. The *hash* function used in the Bitcoin protocol is known as SHA-256 (SHA stands for Secure Hash Algorithm). A cryptographic algorithm with 256 bits of security is seen as highly secure.

A *hash* is like a digital fingerprint; it is unique to each piece of data on the blockchain. Users put information regarding their transaction (name of receiver and sender along with the amount transferred) into a cryptographic *hashing* algorithm—a complex mathematical formula—and receive assets of letters and numbers that are distinct to that transaction. The specific input, if unchanged, will always produce the same exact *hash*. If, however, any part of the data is changed (for example, a malicious actor changes the amount transferred), the *hash* would change to an entirely different set of characters and make it incompatible with the rest of the chain. Therefore, even without seeing the details of the transaction, nodes (computers) can quickly tell that the data within the block has been tampered with and reject that version of the ledger. It is this cryptographic security that makes blockchain ledgers more trustworthy and almost immutable. Example of *hash*: Input *hash* output (using SHA 256 algorithm).

Each *block*/record contains a *cryptographic hash* of the previous *block*/record, a timestamp, and transaction data [Merkle tree where data nodes are represented by leaves]. The Merkle root guarantees the data integrity of the set of transactions tampering with any of them changes its *hash*, which in turn changes all the *hashes* on that branch of the Merkle tree, all the way up to and including the root *hash*.

Since each *block*/record contains information about the previous *block*/record, they effectively form a *chain* with (compare linked data structure), with each additional *block*/record linking to the ones before it. *blockchain* transactions are irreversible in that, once they are recorded, the data in any given *block*/record cannot be altered retroactively without altering all subsequent *blocks*/records. Blockchains Are managed by a peer-to-peer computer network for use as a public distributed ledger, where nodes [a computer or other device that helps maintain a cryptocurrency's *blockchain*s by participating in the transaction] collectively adhere to consensus algorithm protocol to add and validate new transaction *blocks*/records.

In essence, blockchains are important because they allow for new efficiency and reliability in the exchange of valuable and private information that once required a third party to facilitate, such as the movement of money and the validation of identity. Blockchains are powerful tools because they create honest systems that self-correct without the need for a third party to enforce the rules. Blockchains accomplish the enforcement of rules through their consensus algorithm. The consensus is the process of developing an agreement among a group of commonly mistrusting shareholders. These are the full nodes on the network. The full nodes are validating transactions that are entered into the network to be recorded as part of the distributed ledger.

Blueprint of Blockchain

As mentioned earlier, a *blockchain* is a decentralized, distributed, and often public, *digital ledge* consisting of *blocks*/records that are used to record transactions across numerous computers so that any involved *block*/record *cannot* be altered retroactively, without the alteration of all subsequent *blocks*/records. This allows the participants to *verify* and *audit* transactions independently and relatively inexpensively. Its features can increase the transparency and traceability of data and financial assets, facilitate access, and improve the efficiency of transactions.

In brief, blockchain utilizes distributed ledger technology (DLT) to store information verified by cryptography among a group of users, which agreed through a pre-defined network protocol, often without the control of a central authority. The marriage of these technologies gives blockchain networks key characteristics that can remove the need for trust, and therefore enable a secure transfer of value and data directly between parties. Due to this unique ability, blockchain technology can diminish the role of intermediaries, who can command power, collect significant fees, slow economic activity, and are not necessarily trustworthy or altruistic keepers of personal information.

A blockchain database is managed autonomously using a peer-to-peer network and distributed timestamping server. A blockchain has been known as a value-exchange protocol. A blockchain can maintain title rights because, when properly set up to detail the exchange agreement, it provides a record that compels offer and acceptance. In essence, a blockchain can be seen as consisting of several layers—namely, infrastructure, networking [node discovery, information propagation, and verification], consensus [proof of work and proof of stake], data [blocks/records, transactions], application [smart contracts/decentralized applications]

When it comes to *blocks*/records block/record holds batches of valid transactions that are hashed and encoded into a Merkle tree. Each *block*/record includes the cryptographic hash of the prior *block*/record in the blockchain, linking the two. The linked *blocks*/records for a chain. Block time/record time is the average time it takes for the network to generate one extra *block*/record in the blockchain. By the time of *block*/record completion, the included data becomes verifiable.

Blockchain in a Nutshell

Blockchain stores information in batches. It is called *blocks*. These *blocks* are connected together in a sequential way to form a continuous line. Each *block* is like a page of a ledge/record book. Each *block* has three elements—namely, *data, hash,* and *hash of the previous block*.

Blockchain and Cryptocurrency

A blockchain is a data structure that makes it possible to create a *digital ledger* of data and share it among a network. We find there are three different categories of blockchains, namely:

1. Public blockchains. For example, *Bitcoin* is a large distributed network that is run through a *cryptocurrency* which is a *unique* bit of data that can be traded between two parties. These Public blockchains are open for anyone to participate at any level and usually have open-source code.
2. Private blockchains. These are known as *distributed ledger technology* [in short, DLT] They *do not* use a token/cryptocurrency. These tend to be smaller and do not utilize a token or cryptocurrency. The membership of these Private blockchains is closely controlled and is favored by consortiums that have trusted members and trade confidential information.
3. Permissioned blockchains. For example, *ripple* is where individuals can play within the network and are large distributed systems that use a native token.

The above categories of blockchains are contributing to what is known as Web3 [Web 3.0]. Blockchains create permanent records and histories of *transactions*. However, these records are *not* permanent records for that matter. When data is recorded in a blockchain, it is difficult to change or remove it. However, when someone wants to add a record to a blockchain, users in the network who have validation control verify the proposed transaction of the record.

Structure of Blockchain

Each blockchain is *structured* differently. The way that Bitcoin coordinates the organization and input of new data comprises three core *elements*—namely, Block, Chain, and Network.

Block/record: A list of transactions recorded into a ledger over a given period—the size, period, and triggering event for blocks/records is different for every blockchain.

Chain: A hash that links one block to another, mathematically chaining them together.

The hash in the blockchain is created from the data that was in the previous block/record. The hash is a fingerprint of this data and locks blocks/records in order and time.

Network: The network is composed of *full nodes.* Each node contains a complete record of all the transactions that were ever recorded in that blockchain. Nodes (computers) run an algorithm that secures the network. Each node (computer) contains a complete record of all the transactions that were ever recorded in the blockchain. The nodes (computers) are located globally and can be operated by any individual.

In essence, the *blockchain* is a *public ledger* of all transactions in the *Bitcoin network*, and the *nodes* are *computers* that record entries into that ledger. However, *Bitcoin* is the rules that govern this system.

Nodes safeguard the *network* by *mining* for the cryptocurrency *Bitcoin.* New *Bitcoins* are created as a reward for processing transactions and recording them inside the *blockchain.*

How a bunch of *blocks* come together in a *blockchain.* For instance, *Block* 1 contains:

1. *Data* – 10 Bitcoins from you
2. *Hash* – 12A
3. *Previous Hash* – 000

4. *Block* 2 contains:
5. *Data-* 5 Bitcoins from your wife
6. *Hash-* 3B4
7. *Previous Hash*: 12A
8. *Block* 3 contains:
9. *Data* – 4 Bitcoins from your friend
10. *Hash* – C74
11. *Previous Hash* – 3B4

Now, let us see *how* a *blockchain works*:
Block #: 1 < —— > *Block* #: 2 <—> *Block* #: 3

Data – 10 Bitcoins	*Data – 5 Bitcoins*	*Data – 4 Bitcoins*
Hash – 12A	*Hash – 3BA*	*Hash – C74*
Previous Hash -000	*Previous Hash – 12A*	*Previous Hash – 3B4*

Comparison of Bitcoin and Blockchain

The terms *Bitcoin* and *blockchain* are often used interchangeably, but they are *not* the same. *Bitcoin* has a *blockchain.* The Bitcoin blockchain is the underlying protocol that enables the secure transfers of *Bitcoin. Bitcoin* is the name of the *cryptocurrency* that powers the Bitcoin network.

Blockchain is a class of software, and *Bitcoin* is a specific *cryptocurrency. Blockchain* originated with the creation of *Bitcoin. Bitcoins* are powerful tools. Each *blockchain* has its own algorithms for creating agreement within its network on the entries being added.

There are several thousands of blockchains and blockchains-based applications globally in use. These systems allow for the creation of NFT [Non-fungible Token] – the use of cryptocurrency in gaming, faster movement of money through distributed networks, and the development of secure trustworthy applications and hardware.

ICO [Initial Coin Offerings] is another blockchain innovation. They are a type of *smart contract* that allows the issuer to offer a token in exchange for investment funds.

Let us see what a *smart contract* is:

A *smart contract* is a self-executing computer program. This performs pre-defined tasks based upon a predetermined set of criteria/ conditions. These cannot be altered once deployed, their integrity is protected by the public and transparent nature of blockchain. In brief, a smart contact is a tiny computer program that is stored and runs on a blockchain platform. The reason for this is all transactions are completely distributed and no central authority is in control of the money.

Smart contracts can include deadlines that make them useful for time-sensitive transactions and also reduce counterparty risk.

Atomicity and Smart contract: Smart contracts are usually set up such that the entire transaction will fail if any of the multiple steps involved in it cannot be executed.

Smart contracts can facilitate financial transactions. Smart contracts could also be used for commercial transactions. Smart contracts are also called self-executing contracts, blockchain contracts, or digital contracts. Smart contacts remove the intermediary between the buyer and the seller so you can implement things like automatic payments and investment products without the need for a central authority like a bank.

CHAPTER 5

Blockchain Technology—How It Works?

A *blockchain* is a special type of *database*. Blockchain stores information in batches known as *blocks*. These *blocks* are linked together in a sequential way to form a continuous line—a chain of *blocks*/a blockchain. Each *block* is like a page of a ledger/record book. Each *block* has three elements—*data, hash,* and *hash* of the previous block.

Blockchain Technology

The blockchain is a public electronic ledger of all transactions in the Bitcoin network and the nodes are computers that are recording entries into that ledger. The Bitcoin protocol is the rules that govern this system. In brief, blockchain technologies are the *rules* and standards for how an *electronic ledger* is created and maintained; For example, *Bitcoin, Ethereum*, and NXT.

Blockchain technology contains the following concepts:

1. A data store and or database that records changes in the data, the most known are financial transactions.

2. Replication of the data stored across several systems in real time.
3. Peer-to-peer network
4. Digital signatures to provide ownership and authenticity and hashes for references.

The public ledger is known as *blockchain* since once the transactions coming onto the network are grouped into *blocks*/records of data and validated, the *blocks*/records are chained together, and each *block*/record includes a *hash* of the preceding *block*/record, thereby linking them to one another. Thus, each new *block*/record is recurrently linked to all of the preceding *blocks*/records on the chain.

Advantages of Blockchain Technology:

Blockchain has enhanced *digital ledger technology* into a truly decentralized format that eliminates the need for a trusted intermediary to process and validate transactions between two parties. The transactions ledger cannot be overridden, hacked, or manipulated.

Blockchain Technology in a Nutshell

Blockchain technology is being used as the basis for all types of secure transactions from secure information exchange to smart contracts and more. At its simplest, a blockchain is an encrypted network used to store, distribute and generate information. The basic storage unit for information on the blockchain is a set of transactions known as a *block*. All the *blocks* on a blockchain are related to one another. Changing information on a given *block* would break the chain- and every computer [node] on the network would know about it. Each *block* is protected with complex encryption. As *blocks* get linked, they create a permanent transaction history visible to the entire network. Since they are decentralized, there is no intermediary overseeing the transaction database. No single user can override or alter the blockchain's history. That makes it an extremely secure system.

Decentralized applications (dAPP) can manage digital assets and decentralized autonomous organizations (DAO). DAOs are a type of Ethereum application that represents a virtual entity within Ethereum. When you create a DAO, you can invite others to participate in the governance of the organization.

DAO membership structure:

Token-based membership, Share-based membership, and Reputation-based membership.

This is the second-largest digital currency after Bitcoin. Ethereum is a decentralized software platform that enables the development of contracts and decentralized apps.

How Decentralized Autonomous Organizations [DAO] work:

1. A group of people writes a *smart contract* to govern the organization.
2. People add funds to the DAO and are given tokens that represent ownership.
3. This structure works like stock in a company, but the members have control of the funds from day one.
4. When the funds have been raised, the DAO begins to operate by having members propose how to spend the money. Voting may be affected by how much *Ether* the member risks or stakes in the DAO.
5. The members vote on these proposals.
6. When the predetermined time has passed and the predetermined number of votes has accrued, the proposal passes or fails.
7. Individuals act as contractors to service the DAO.

CHAPTER 6

Knowledge of Digital Ledger Technology and Ethereum

Digital Ledger Technology

Digital Ledger Technology [DLT] is the technological infrastructure and protocols that allow simultaneous access, validation, and record updating across a networked *database*. In essence, Digital Ledger Technology is a *database* that is consensually shared and synchronized across multiple sites, institutions, or countries accessible by multiple people. In brief, distributed ledgers are maintained by a network of nodes/computers that has a copy of the ledgers, validates the information, and helps reach a consensus about its accuracy.

Digital Ledger technology enables secure, transparent, and decentralized transactions *without* the need for *central authority*. DLT is used to create secure, and tamper-proof digital identity. It also can be used to create a secure and transparent *voting system* that can prevent *voter fraud* and ensure the integrity of the voting process. Digital Ledger Technology allows for smart contracts, programs that automatically execute/complete based on prevailing conditions. It can be used to record property transactions.

Ethereum

Ethereum has a public blockchain running on several thousand computers and the token on the blockchain is known as *Ether*. Ethereum is a bunch of *protocols* written out as *codes* which is run as Ethereum software which creates Ethereum transactions containing data about Ether coins [ETH] recorded on Ethereum blockchain.

The main Ethereum network is a public, permissionless network where any individual can download and write software to connect to the network and start creating transactions and smart contracts, validate them, and mining *blocks/*records without needing to sign up with any others.

It is an open-source crowdfunded project that built the Ethereum blockchains. Ethereum network allows anyone to create smart contracts, create decentralized organizations, and deploy decentralized applications.

Let us see how the *Ethereum network* works:

To participate in the Ethereum network, Ethereum client software has to be utilized. Ethereum client software can be used to connect to the Ethereum network, validate transactions and *blocks/* records, create new transactions, create smart contracts, and run smart contracts [as a matter of fact, Ethereum smart contracts are *short programs* that are stored on Ethereum's blockchain, replicated across all the nodes and are available for any individual to inspect] and mine for new *blocks/*records.

Then the computer becomes a *node* on the network, running an *Ethereum Virtual Machine* [EVM], and becomes equivalent to all other nodes. EVM processes all the Ethereum transactions and *blocks/*records and keeps track of all the account balances and results of the smart contracts. Each node on the Ethereum network runs the same EVM and processes the same data, resulting in them all having the same view.

In essence, Ethereum client software will connect over the Internet to other people's computers running similar client software and start downloading the Ethereum blockchain from them to catch up with the latest state of the blockchain. It will validate that each *block*/record conforms to the Ethereum protocol rules.

Ethereum token is known as *Ether* [ETH]. This cryptocurrency can be traded for other currencies like Bitcoin.

Let us see the Ethereum blockchain ecosystem:

To set up an Ethereum wallet:

1. Go to www. Ethreum.org.
2. Click the download button.
3. Open the Ethereum wallet.
4. Choose Develop from the drop-down menu.
5. Select one of the tests networks.
6. Create a strong password.
7. Click through the startup menu.
8. Choose Develop —> Start Mining

DAO [Decentralized Autonomous Organization]. These are a type of Ethereum application that represents a virtual entity within Ethereum.

To build DAO:

1. Go to www.ethereum.org/dao.
2. Scroll down the page to the Code box and copy the code.
3. Open the Ethereum wallet.
4. Develop your DAO in the Ethereum wallet.

How the *Ethereum network* works:

To participate in the Ethereum network, Ethereum client software has to be utilized. Ethereum client software can be used to connect the Ethereum network, validate transactions and blocks/records, create new transactions, create *smart contracts*, and run *smart contracts* [*note*: Ethereum *smart contacts* are short programs that are stored on

Ethereum's *blockchain*, replicated across all the nodes and are available for any individual to inspect] and mine for new blocks/records.

Then the computer becomes a node on the network, running an Ethereum Virtual Machine [EVM], and becomes equivalent to all other nodes. EVM processes all the Ethereum transactions and blocks/records and keeps track of all the account balances and results of the *smart contracts*. Each node on the Ethereum network runs the same EVM and processes the same data, resulting in them all having the same view.

In essence, Ethereum client software will connect over the Internet to other people's computers running similar client software and start downloading the Ethereum *blockchain* from them to catch up with the latest state of the *blockchain*. It will validate that each block/record conforms to the Ethereum protocol rules.

Ethereum Blockchain Ecosystem

To set up an *Ethereum wallet*:

1. Go to www.Ethreum.org.
2. Click the download button.
3. Open the Ethereum wallet.
4. Choose Develop from the drop-down menu.
5. Select one of the test networks.
6. Create a strong password.
7. Click through the startup menu.
8. Choose develop —> Start mining.

CHAPTER 7

Knowledge of Tokens

Tokens are a digital representation of an asset or utility in a *blockchain*. They usually reside on top of another *blockchain* rather than their own independent *blockchain*. Tokens are meant to serve a different purpose to money, which is what coins and altcoins are all about. They can represent any asset that is fungible. Being fungible means that you can replace it with an identical item. For instance, you can interchange your 100-dollar bill for any other 100-dollar bill. This makes it fungible.

A Token represents a fungible or tradeable asset or utility that resides on a blockchain, the technology behind cryptocurrencies. They are essentially the representation of each individual cryptocurrency and are created and distributed through a token contract. The terms *crypto coin* or *crypto token* are often used interchangeably. However, it is important to note that a *token* and a *coin* are different things.

Coins are a form of digital currency that are native to a *blockchain* and work as a medium of exchange whereas A *token* is a digital asset that uses smart contact to serve a variety of functions. Coins represent value whereas tokens represent utility.

Knowledge of *tokens*:

A *Token* in cryptocurrency is a digital representation of an asset/ interest in something and is built on a *blockchain*. It can be utilized as *investments*, to store value to make purchases. *Tokens* live on existing *blockchains*, for example, *Ethereum* or *Binance* Smart chain and are built utilizing their infrastructure.

Purpose of *Token*:

It facilitates *transactions* on a *blockchain* but represents an investor's stake in a business/company or serves an economic purpose. However, *tokens* are *not* legal tender. In other words, *token* holders can use them to make purchases/trades like *securities* to make a profit.

Token Contract

A token contract is a smart contract that maps account addresses and balances. A token contract and a token contract are different. Crypto tokens represent a unit of value whereas a token's contract addresses are the location of the actual token contract.

CHAPTER 8

Knowledge of Non-Fungible Tokens (NFT)

Non-fungible Tokens (NFT) are unique cryptocurrency tokens that exist on a *blockchain* and cannot be replicated. NFTs represent assets anything from digital art to videos that have been tokenized through a *blockchain*. These are unique ID cards. NFTs are created via a process called *minting*. The assets' information gets encrypted and recorded on the *blockchain*. They are *not* interchangeable. NFTs can be created directly on NFT platforms, allowing you to *mint*—the process of creating and uploading your artwork on a *blockchain*.

An NFT is a digital asset that cannot be duplicated or changed. NFTs are a type of cryptographic token that represents unique assets in both the real and digital worlds. They act as a verification of authenticity and ownership for items within *blockchain* networks. In order to be non-fungible, NFTs must:

1. Not be interchangeable
2. Not be divisible
3. Not be able to be duplicated
4. Be unique
5. Be immutable/permanent and unalterable

NFTs contain unique information. This information is recorded in a smart contract on a *blockchain*. This makes each individual NFT unique. They cannot be replaced or swapped with another token because no two NFTs are ever identical.

There are different types of NFTs that give us the ability to effectively tokenize things such as the following:

1. Artwork
2. Collectibles
3. Gaming assets
4. Virtual fashion
5. Event tickets
6. Music and audio content

How NFTs work:

NFTs are created and stored on a *blockchain*. The ownership of an NFT is established and recorded on a *blockchain* network. Proof of ownership is an important part of NFTs. This is because it proves that you own the original and authentic copy of a digital file.

Many different *blockchains* support NFTs. For instance, Ethereum is the overall leader among other *blockchain* networks and NFTs were originally born on Ethereum *blockchain*. Due to its data structure, Ethereum is a highly secure network, and the majority of NFT projects run on the Ethereum *blockchain* in the form of ERC-721 coins/tokens. Although Ethereum is the leading *blockchain* in support of NFTs, there are also many others, such as Solana and Cardano.

CHAPTER 9

How to Invest in Cryptocurrencies?

The easiest way to purchase cryptocurrencies is to go directly through an online cryptocurrency exchange platform. By doing so on decentralized exchanges, you will eliminate third-party interference in your transaction.

The most popular cryptocurrency exchanges are as follows:

Centralized cryptocurrency exchange [CEX]:

These are similar to traditional stock exchanges. These buyers and sellers come together, and exchange plays the role of an intermediary. These exchanges charge a commission to facilitate the transactions made between the buyers and the sellers. The centralize means *to trust somebody else to handle the money.*

How a CEX works:

1. You give your money to the exchange.
2. The exchange holds it for you like a bank or trusted intermediary.
3. You watch the prices of the available cryptocurrencies on the exchange.
4. Depending on the exchange, you can trade your fiat currency—a traditional currency such as the US dollar for a

cryptocurrency such as Bitcoin. With most exchanges, you find better luck exchanging two currencies for one another.
5. You place your order.
6. The exchange finds you a seller to match your buy order. If you are selling, the exchange finds you a buyer.

One of the most popular centralized exchanges that offers fiat/cryptocurrency pairings is *Binance.* It supports more than seven hundred cryptocurrencies worldwide. It is one of the cheapest platforms to use as transaction fees are pretty low.

The other centralized exchange is *Coinbase*. It is one of the most beginner-friendly cryptocurrency exchange platforms and offers basic transactions, a digital wallet, and easy withdrawals. It supports over two hundred cryptocurrencies and is insured up to $250,000. It also offers a Visa debit card that is accepted by over fifty million merchants globally.

Decentralized cryptocurrency exchanges [DEX]:

It does not rely on an intermediary to hold your funds. It is a marketplace where buyers and sellers come together and process transactions directly between one another. DEXs facilitate peer-to-peer trades. On a DEX, you can buy and sell your cryptocurrency assets directly from other market participants. You would be able to make the deals through things like smart contracts. DEXs are harder to hack than CXs. Most DXs do not offer services to deposit or withdraw fiat currencies such as the US Dollar.

There are popular DXs such as *Curve* [Ethereum], DODOP, CakeSwap, and Uniswap.

Hybrid cryptocurrency exchanges:

This exchange platform gives you access to *private keys* and allows you to trade for a lower fee. It provides cryptocurrency trading services with speed, ease, and liquidity to institutional users. A hybrid exchange connects its centralized elements to a network of decentralized elements. Hybrids are also known as semi-decentralized exchanges because they incorporate both on-chain and off-chain components. An example of a hybrid exchange is *Qurrex*.

How to Select an Exchange Platform?

Security is one of the topmost issues in the cryptocurrency industry. Exchanges are usually the risk of hacking and fraudulent activities. Moreover, there are individuals who encourage investors to buy a crypto asset in order to artificially inflate its value and then sell their own assets at high prices.

There are four safety features you must check on the exchange:

1. Two-factor authentication [2FA] – It is a method of confirming your claimed identity by using a combination of two different factors—something the exchange knows like your password and something it has like a six-digit number it sends to your email/smartphone for the second step of the verification.
2. Multifactor authentication [MFA] – It is an authentication method that requires the user to provide two or more verification factors to gain access to a resource such as an application, online account, or a VPN. It is a secure way to make sure that someone is who they say they are. They need to give two things that show it is them. For example, their name and password.
3. Cold storage for the majority of funds – The exchange stores your funds offline, so the risk of online hacking is lower.
4. Proof of reserve – It requires the exchange to be audited to verify that the total amount of funds held by the exchange matches the amount required to cover an anonymized set of customer balances.

Liquidity:

After you decide which cryptocurrencies you want to purchase, make sure your exchange offers sufficient liquidity and trading volume for fast and easy transactions. Liquidity also ensures you are able to buy and sell without the cryptocurrency's price being significantly affected by big market movers. The more buyers and sellers there are, the more liquidity that exists. The best way to measure an exchange's liquidity is to look up its most recent trading volume.

Charging Fees:

The most common method is taking a small percentage of the amount you trade. Most exchanges charge a low percentage to stay competitive, some exchanges go as low as around 0.2 %.

Easy-to-use:

This factor depends upon what kind of device you want to use for your cryptocurrency investing activities. This is important for new beginners.

Location:

Keep in mind issues like which fiat currency exchanges accept and what fees they charge locals compared to international customers. The location of the exchange dictates the laws it has to comply with.

Payment method:

Some exchanges require deposits by bank transfer, some use PayPal, and some accept credit and debit cards.

Customer support:

You can check this factor either by directly contacting the customer support department and asking questions that you have not been able to find on the exchange's FAQ page or by perusing online cryptocurrency forums.

Trading options:

These are important for active and advanced traders. For instance, depending on your risk tolerance and financial goals, you may want to have access to certain order types or margin trading.

Transaction limits:

Most exchanges have a daily withdrawals/deposit limit. These limits are something you may need to keep in mind depending on your investing style and goals.

How to Invest in Cryptocurrency Coins in Five Steps

Before you can purchase your cryptocurrency coin, you will need a place to keep it. In other words, you'll have to have a Cryptocurrency Wallet. Conveniently, most exchange platforms offer a default wallet that you can use. You can also buy your own cold wallet and direct your coins to it.

The next step is to find a reputable exchange platform to purchase your cryptocurrency coin. Before you sign up with an exchange platform check to see that it supports your preferred method of payment and whether you will have to pay extra to use it. Many exchange platforms charge fees for certain payment methods, like international wire transfers or credit card transactions.

Once you have chosen an exchange platform, the next step is to create an account and verify your identity. This process will likely include your personal information, like a copy of your driver's license and proof of address. This process can also take several days, so you may have to be patient.

Decide how much you want to invest. The majority of cryptocurrencies like Bitcoin can cost tens of thousands of dollars per coin. Fortunately, you don't have to buy them in round numbers. So, whether you decide to buy a bunch of coins that cost less than a dollar, like Dogecoin, or a tiny fraction of a pricier crypto like Bitcoin or Ether, you can keep your investment to a reasonable size.

Once you have selected an exchange platform, set up an account, and decide how much you want to spend, you are ready to make your purchase. You can use the coins in your digital wallet at more than 15,000 businesses worldwide or keep them as an investment and hope they grow. If you don't want to go through an exchange platform, or you want to convert cash to coins, another option is Bitcoin

ATM. Insert cash, and the ATM will give you a QR code that you can use to send the coins directly to your digital wallet.

A person has to go through a *cryptocurrency exchange platform* such as *Coinbase* using CashAPP or go through *broker*-dealers and sign up/fund for their account and start trading.

Financial derivatives such as *Bitcoin futures* and *Bitcoin trusts* and ETFs are available, for instance, CME [Chicago Mercantile Exchange] offers *Bitcoin futures. Bitcoin trusts* and ETFs allow you to indirectly invest in *Bitcoins* without holding it. They are usually traded on traditional stock exchanges.

There are mining companies involved in mining and maintaining the *blockchain* network. There are companies supporting cryptocurrency such as Robinhood and PayPal that facilitate cryptocurrency transactions.

STEPS TO BUY CRYPTOCURRENCY FROM AN EXCHANGE

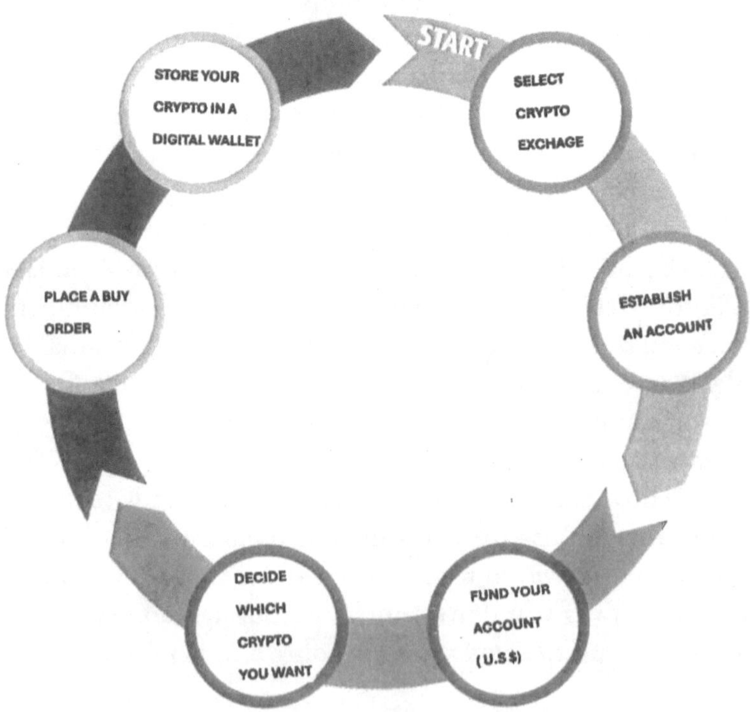

Guidelines for Investing Cryptocurrencies:

1. Never invest more than you can afford to lose.
2. Use dollar-cost averaging for cryptocurrency.
3. *Research* and stick to the fundamentals.
4. Stick to the *major cryptocurrencies.*
5. Use *safe* storage—Hardware wallet.
6. Maintain a balanced portfolio.
7. Take the time to understand *blockchain technology.*
8. Follow *new* laws/regulatory developments related to *cryptocurrency.*
9. Use technical indicators to form decision-making such as *moving averages*, *relative strengths*, etc.
10. Remain flexible and open to *new information* on *cryptocurrency investments.*

How to invest safely in cryptocurrency:

The safest place to invest in cryptocurrency is on an exchange platform where virtual coins are bought and sold by many people. On exchange platforms, you can buy coins with fiat money like dollars and sell them for dollars, or trade between cryptocurrencies. Some exchange platforms are also known for other services, like the online brokerage Robinhood and PayPal.

Experts recommend sticking to large popular exchange platforms such as Binance, Coinbase, FTX, and Kraken.

Dividends of cryptocurrencies are as follows:

Proof-of-stake: Staking and getting passive income from cryptocurrency is a lighter version of proof-of-work in cryptocurrency mining. In brief, when you stake a cryptocurrency, it means you put it aside so it cannot be used in the blockchain network. If you have many stakes, you have a higher chance of getting paid at a random selection by the network. Annual returns for staking vary between one percent to five percent, depending on the coin.

Hodling: Buying and holding the tokens of a cryptocurrency exchange that pays dividends in cryptocurrency. Some cryptocurrencies pay out the *hodlers*, who simply purchase and carry the digital coins in their wallets.

Exchange-Traded Funds [ETF]: Cryptocurrency allows investors to gain exposure to the cryptocurrency market without directly purchasing and storing digital assets. Exchange-traded funds track the price performance of cryptocurrencies by investing in portfolios linked to their instruments. Cryptocurrency Exchange-Traded Funds on regular stock exchanges and investors can hold them in their standard brokerage accounts.

Investing in ICOs (Initial Coin Offerings)

ICOs are like fundraising for a ness rat-up, except that your new ideas revolve around a new *cryptocurrency* rather than a business idea or product. In other words, you are trying to raise money in the form of other, already-established cryptocurrencies such as Bitcoin and Ethereum. An ICO is crowdfunding, using other cryptocurrencies, for a new cryptocurrency that is connected to a product.

How ICO works:

1. Create white paper. It is a detailed document explaining a business model and the reason a particular coin may really take off.
2. Add a tab to your website dedicated to the OCO funding.
3. Spread the word to your connections and ask for funding.
4. Sell a quantity of your crowdfunded coin in the form of tokens, which means digital assets.
5. Send the investors coin tokens.

Cryptocurrency taxes:

You are likely to get taxed when being exposed to *cryptocurrencies* if you are doing the following:

1. Selling cryptocurrencies for a fiat currency such as the US dollar.

2. Trading one cryptocurrency for another.
3. Using cryptocurrency to buy goods or services.

There are some cryptocurrency tax experts:

1. Camuso CPA
2. Crypto Tax Girl

Countries where cryptocurrencies are in circulation:

1. Vietnam
2. Philippines
3. Ukraine
4. India
5. USA
6. Pakistan
7. Brazil
8. Thailand
9. Russia
10. China
11. Nigeria
12. Turkey
13. Argentina
14. Morocco
15. UK
16. Ecuador
17. El Salvador
18. Kenya
19. Indonesia
20. UAE
21. Singapore
22. Venezuela
23. South Africa
24. Germany
25. Canada

Popular Cryptocurrencies around the globe:

1. Bitcoin (BTC)
2. Ethereum (ETH)
3. Tether (USDT)
4. Binance Coin (BNB)
5. USD Coin (USDC)

World's Largest *Exchange Platforms* for Cryptocurrencies:

1. Bitcoin
2. Coinbase
3. Kraken
4. Kucoin
5. Bybit

2024 Top Cryptocurrencies in the World:

1. Bitcoin
2. Bitcoin Cash [BCH]
3. Bitcoin SV [BSV]
4. BITDAO [BIT]
5. BitTorrent-New [BTT]
6. Ethereum (ETH)
7. Ethereum Classic [ETC]
8. EthereumPow [ETHW]
9. Tether [USDT]
10. Biance USD [BUSD]
11. U. S. Dollar coin (USDC)
12. XRP
13. Cardano [ADA]
14. Dogecoin [DOGE]
15. Polygon [MATIC]
16. Polkadot [DOT]
17. Solana [SOL]
18. Dai [DAI]

19. Shiba Inu [SHIB]
20. TRON [TRX]
21. Avalanche [AVAX]
22. Uniswap [UNI]
23. Litecoin [LTC]
24. Wrapped Bitcoin [WBTC]
25. UNUS SED LEO [LEO]
26. Chainlink [LINK]
27. Cosmos [ATOM]
28. Stellar [XLM]
29. Lido DAO
30. Aptos (Apt)
31. Compound (Comp)
32. Monero [XMR]
33. Cronos [CRO]
34. Algorand [ALGO]
35. Near Protocol [NEAR]
36. Toncoin [TON]
37. VeChain [VET]
38. Quant [QNT]
39. Filecoin [FIL]
40. Terra Classic [LUNC]
41. Flow [FLOW]
42. Chiliz [CHZ]
43. OKB [OKB]
44. Hedera [HBAR]
45. Internet Computer [ICP]
46. MultiversX [Elrond]
47. ApeCoin [APE]
48. Tezos [XTZ]
49. Theta Network [THETA]
50. Huobi Token [HT]
51. The Sandbox [SAND]
52. Aave [AAVE]
53. Decentraland [MANA]
54. EOS [EOS]

55. Pax Dollar [USDP]
56. Chain [XCN]
57. Gemini Dollar [GUSD]
58. KuCoin Token [KCS]
59. TrueUSD [TUSD]
60. Maker [MKR]
61. Axe Infinity [AXS]
62. USDD [USDD]
63. Aptos [AXS]
64. PancakeSwap [CAKE]
65. IOTA [MIOTA]
66. Neutrino USD [USDN]
67. Synthetix [SNX]
68. eCash [XEC]
69. Zcash [ZEC]
70. PAX Gold [PAXG]
71. Klaytn [KLAY]
72. Fantom [FTM]
73. Neo [NEO]
74. The Graph [GRT]
75. Trust Wallet [TWT]
76. Nexo [NEXO]
77. Mina [MINA]
78. Gate Token [GT]
79. FTX Token [FTT]
80. FEI USD [FEI]
81. BinaryX [BNX]
82. Basic Attention Token [BAT]
83. THORChain [RUNE]
84. Dash [DASH]
85. Helium [HNT]
86. Curve DAO Token [CRV]
87. Lido DAO [LDO]
88. Enjin Coin [ENJ]
89. Loopring [LRC]
90. Casper [CSPR]

91. Osmosis [OSMO]
92. Arweave [AR]
93. 1inch Network [1 INCH]
94. ImmutableX [IMX]
95. Zilliqa [ZIL]
96. XDC Network [XDC]
97. Stacks [STX]
98. Decred [DCR]
99. NEM [XEM]
100. KAVA [KAVA]
101. Ripple [XRP]
102. Render Token (RNDR)
103. Singularity Net (AGIX)
104. Injective (INJ)
105. Conflux (CFX)

CHAPTER 10

Future of Global Financial Systems

Cryptocurrency in terms of the Global financial system:

Cryptocurrency is having an enormous impact on the global financial system. It is challenging traditional institutions and creating new opportunities for financial innovation. In other words, the rise of cryptocurrency has been driven by several factors such as decentralization, security, and potential for innovation.

One of the most significant developments has been the rise of decentralized finance [DeFi]. This has created several new opportunities for financial innovation and has the potential to challenge the traditional financial system. In essence, cryptocurrency has disrupted traditional financial institutions by providing an alternative to the centralized financial system. The global financial system encompasses financial markets and current markets in the world economy. Besides these, exchange rates and capital flows among those nations wrap them together. However, they face more problems than benefits. In brief, developing nations feel that they are manipulated in favor of the developed nations around the world. We also see fintech, decentralized finance [DeFi], even central bank digital currency [CBDC], and other new advanced technologies will pave the way to transform the global financial system.

Blockchain technology and Digital Ledger Technology [DLT] in terms of Global Financial System:

We see that cryptocurrency and digital ledger technology will become a major player in the global financial system and that it will play a crucial role in shaping the future of money and finance. Blockchain and digital ledger technology are advancing rapidly and more people adopt them. In fact, blockchain technologies are connecting the global financial system. They are easily interoperable, efficient, affordable, and accessible. They can reduce the cost and time of cross-border payments. In essence, blockchain technology reduces fraud, ensures quick and secure transactions, and trading, and it helps to manage risk within the interconnected global financial system. With blockchain technology, anyone can connect financial infrastructure anywhere in the world. Digital ledger technology is a decentralized database that records transactions in a secure and transparent manner. It has the potential to revolutionize the global financial system by enabling faster, cheaper, and more secure transactions.

When it comes to digital ledger technology, it decentralizes critical data and enables an entirely new financial system where capital flows without the need for traditional intermediaries such as banks. Digital ledger technology offers the potential for tracking various stages of trade and financial transactions.

The era of cash / credit card / debit card etc. is coming to an end and that of CBDC—Central Bank Digital Currencies has already begun with *digital* payment systems becoming the criterion around the globe. We see many of the global population are gaining access to digital systems. In other words, fintech is transforming the world of finance.

The future of cryptocurrency in global financial systems will be shaped by regulations as the role of government regulators in the world will be a foremost important factor in the future of cryptocurrency. Central banks and government regulators have their eyes on this growing trend in the crypto space. There will be an impact on the development of the global financial system in terms of crypto space in the years to come. Blockchain will play a crucial role.

The future of global financial systems has been intellectually impacted by cryptocurrencies. For instance, transactions, financial inclusion, and funding have been altered by their cross-border nature, decentralization, and potential innovation. In essence, cryptocurrencies can enable financial inclusion by creating open democratic financial systems that are global, open source, and accessible to all who have access to the Internet, regardless of nationality, ethnicity, race, gender, and socioeconomic class.

We see most of the global financial institutions carry corruption and incompetence on a grand scale. It is in a state of upheaval disrupting honest human enterprise the systems. When Bitcoin was created, it showed that building a non-hackable system of rules utilizing software known as *blockchain* is possible without anyone making it work. It showed that the digital system could be applied to law and private ownership of labor, merchandise, property, and financial institutions and how they work. Bitcoin showed that users of all systems can deal honestly and openly between two individuals and that administrator is unnecessary.

In essence, Bitcoin is an immutable system of truth that can be utilized to conduct transactions around the globe without ever being exposed to the monopolies that have previously served as go-between-taking fees. We find decentralized finance (DeFi) is challenging the need for bureaucracies in financial services. There is a software NFT [Non-fungible Tokens] that has systems of rules to eliminate issues and deal honestly and truthfully with others without the need for many bureaucracies.

Blockchain technology will get rid of most of the abusive monopolies. It is estimated that 1.7 billion people globally still do not have access to banking institutions or cannot afford banking services. Now, they depend on cryptocurrency to join free commerce.

Global financial systems, particularly in the banking industry, were the first to recognize the threat of *Bitcoin* and then the potential of *Blockchain technology* to transform the industry. The *digital currency* does not carry the *cost* of handling cash and that is traceable as it moves through the *financial system.*

One of the primary challenges that the United States faces is that it's decentralized in the distribution of power and decision-making. Each county and each state will come up with its own rules for how to implement or use blockchain technology.

Ninety-five (95%) of the global population has access to *cryptocurrencies*. In other words, they can buy and trade new financial products. In essence, every individual could start using a sovereign identity [sovereign identity refers to an individual's ability to control and manage their own digital identity, instead of relying on third parties to do so on their behalf.

In other words, a sovereign identity system, which may include personal information, credentials, and other types of data. These identities are usually stored on a decentralized platform, such as blockchain, which allows the public to control and access their identity information without relying upon a central authority. In essence, the goal of sovereign identity is to give individuals more control over their personal data and to enable them to securely and privately interact with various systems and services online.

Lately, we see Decentralized finance (DeFi) is counterbalanced to transform the global financial systems. Many countries around the globe are currently developing new blockchain-based technologies, platforms, and applications that offer alternatives to traditional financial services. In essence, many of these businesses are transforming the way people store, transfer, and manage their money, making finance accessible, secure, and efficient. These businesses are being created to make decentralized (DeFi) a reality for people around the globe.

The growing ecosystem of cryptocurrency is making headways into the global financial systems. Globally, the number of users of various cryptocurrencies has grown to more than 100 million. As Blockchain technology develops, more private and public sectors around the world acknowledge and accept cryptocurrency as a viable global financial system.

About five years ago, the deputy governor of Sweden's central bank, predicted the end of money. She said, "If you extrapolate current trends, the last note will have been handed back to the Riksbank (Sweden) by the year 2030."

What she meant was the use of paper currency to carry out commercial transactions in Sweden would cease at that point. As a matter of fact, the Sverige's Riksbank was the world's first central bank and among the first to issue currency banknotes.

Now we see smartphones allow us to conduct banking and financial transactions no matter where we are. Consumers around the globe are faced with a range of important transformations, which they are adopting with varying degrees of enthusiasm depending on their age, technical savvy, and socioeconomic status. Companies/businesses around the world are having to adapt as well. All these revolutionary transformations in finance seemed to have been heralded. In brief, there are numerous cryptocurrencies available in the world.

These currencies have been heralded as a replacement for fiat currency. In this scenario, cryptocurrencies would disrupt the global financial system so completely that they will supplant all conventional currencies, even the dollar, sterling, yen, yuan, etc.

CHAPTER 11

Worldwide Exchange/ Trading Platforms

There are about 25,000 *cryptocurrencies* in circulation with a total market capitalization of $1.5 trillion, and there are about 11,000 active *cryptocurrencies.*

There are 650–700 million cryptocurrencies ownership around the globe. This is a significant growth of 35–40 % since 2023.

Sixty-five percent are *male*, and 35% are *female.* Seventy-five percent are under thirty-four years old.

Governments around the globe are working to integrate *cryptocurrencies* into their mainstream economy.

Cryptocurrency ownership continental-wise:

1. *Asia* is around 400–500 million
2. *North America* is 80–100 million
3. *South America* is 60–70 million
4. *Europe* is 50–70 million
5. *Africa* is 45–50 million
6. *Australia/New Zealand* is 4–6 million

Percentage of Cryptocurrency Ownership:

1. *India*: 8–10%
2. *China*: 7–11%
3. *United States of America*: 27–30%
4. *Vietnam*: 25–40%
5. *Pakistan*: 10–12%
6. *Philippines*: 20–35%
7. *Brazil*: 10–12%
8. *Nigeria*: 33–35%
9. *Indonesia*: 10–15%
10. *Iran*: 15–20%
11. *Russia*: 12–13%
12. *Thailand*: 20–25%
13. *Saudi Arabia*: 18–25%
14. *South Africa*: 10–20%
15. *Japan*: 5–11%
16. *Ethiopia*: 5–8%
17. *Turkey*: 16–20%
18. *Mexico*: 4–8%
19. *Bangladesh*: 2–6%
20. *France*: 28–30%
21. *Ukraine*: 12–30%
22. *United Kingdom*: 11–20%
23. *Germany*: 5–15%
24. *Egypt*: 3–7%
25. *Venezuela*: 11–18%
26. *Kenya*: 5–15%
27. *United Arab Emirates*: 25–40%
28. *Argentina*: 10–30%
29. *Colombia*: 5–8%
30. *South Korea*: 4–11%
31. *Morocco*: 5–11%
32. *DR Congo*: 24%
33. *Canada*: 5–15%
34. *Tanzania*: 3–5%

35. *Italy*: 5–10%
36. *Spain*: 3–8%
37. *Nepal*: 5–8%
38. *Poland*: 3–8%
39. *Malaysia*: 4–7%
40. *Algeria*: 3–5%
41. *Peru*: 15–17%
42. *Singapore*: 15–30%
43. *Iraq*: 2–5%
44. *Myanmar*: 2–4%
45. *Ghana*: 3–4%
46. *Australia*: 4–8%
47. *Ecuador*: 5–8%
48. *Mozambique*: 2–5%
49. *Cambodia*: 4–7%
50. *Uganda*: 2–4%

Cryptos World

Visit/view: crypto.com

Antigua and Barbada

Cryptocurrency: Financial innovation in cryptocurrency and blockchain technologies. Bitcoin and bitcoin cash is accepted.

Regulation: There are no limits for foreign control investments and ownership. Foreign investors may hold up to 100 % of an investment. Mostly legal investment.

Population: 102,634

Business Culture Characteristics: Handshaking is the normal greeting for acquaintances and a formal introduction. Business cards are exchanged.

Literacy: 99%

Economy: Dual island—tourism and construction-driven economy—limited water supply.

GDP per capita: $29,000

Argentina

Regulation: Mostly legal investment

Cryptocurrency: Cryptocurrency is accepted. Cryptocurrency exchange platforms are Binance, Bitex, and Satoshi Tango.

Population: 47,000,000

Business Culture Characteristics: Argentine people tend to differ from other Latin Americans in the way they conduct business. They are seen as resourceful, highly educated, and motivated to form business networks and boost the exchange between Argentina and the rest of the world. The business style in Argentina is colored by the mixed heritage that it has. Generally, they are intensely competitive, and this has been one of the redeeming factors that have increased the internationalization of their markets; Family-oriented; Personal relationships; Loyalty to individual people; And high value placed on educational level.

The Argentines emphasize the individual's role in society and view the individual who is independent as capable. This affects the business culture since the Argentines perceive one who takes orders from another as weak and inadequate. Acts of generosity, which manifest in helping someone in need, are considered an exercise of free will.

The difference between the residents of Buenos Aires and the rest of the country is also an aspect of culture that should be noted. When dealing with an Argentine, it is important to note their frankness in voicing out their opinions, though they take extreme care in being diplomatic. Their warm nature and friendliness are seen in situations when they try to establish a personal relationship prior to business dealings.

It is also important to note the concept of space and time in dealing with Argentina. Most Argentines maintain little physical distance between speakers and tend to broach personal issues pertaining to the family in their conversation. Time is considered to be an asset to be enjoyed rather than utilized, and most Argentines take this to be useful in establishing relationships and clarifying situations better.

The role of the family in Argentine life is to be emphasized. Family is deemed central to the life of the average citizen, and filial piety and bonds to elders are cherished. However, one of the main perils of working in Argentina would be in dealing with nepotism. Most positions are filled with family members first, and while there are specific rules that limit such incidents, this occurrence is significantly less than in other Latin American countries.

Literacy: 99%

Economy: Large and diversified economy.

GDP: $26,500

Australia

Regulation: Mostly legal investment.

Cryptocurrency: Cryptocurrency accepted. Cryptocurrency exchange platforms are Bybit, Swyfix, Coinspot, Coinjar, Luno, eToro, Binance, Kucoin, Phemex, and Cointree.

Population: 26,768,598

Business Culture Characteristics: Australians tend to be friendly and easygoing. This behavior does not carry over to business relations. Most expect a code of etiquette with emphasis on the verbal as well as nonverbal aspects. It is considered appropriate to offer your business card, but you might not receive one in return because most Australians do not carry name cards. It is customary to shake hands when greeting, as it is at the conclusion of a meeting. It is also acceptable for people to introduce themselves without waiting to be introduced, and most Australians would perceive this as informal and outgoing.

Literacy: 99%

Economy: Strong financial sector, energy investor.

GDP per capita: $60,000

Austria

Regulation: Mostly legal investment.

Cryptocurrency: Cryptocurrency is accepted. Binance, Kraken, and Bitpanda are the cryptocurrency exchange platforms.

Population: 8,967,982

Business Culture Characteristics: Meticulous attention, punctuality, dress code is formal.

Literacy: 99%
Economy: One of the strongest in EU and Euro economies.
GDP: $64,600

Bangladesh

Regulation: Prohibits

Cryptocurrency: Cryptocurrency exchange platforms are Binance, eToro

Population: 168,697,184

Business Culture Characteristics: Arrive for meetings on time, handshaking, exchange business cards, professionalism is highly valued.

Literacy: 74.9%

Economy: One of the fastest growing economies.

GDP: $8,200

Belgium

Regulation: Mostly legal investment

Cryptocurrency: Legal. Cryptocurrency exchange platforms are Uphold, Bybit, Binance, Bitpanda, and Crypto.com

Population: 11,977,634

Business Culture Characteristics: Hierarchical. Job titles and ranks are important; Meetings are formal; Decision-making is slow; Appointments should be made in advance.

Literacy: 99%

Economy: High-income economy

GDP: $63,600

Belarus

Regulation: Mostly legal investment.

Cryptocurrency: Cryptocurrency is accepted. Binance, Kraken, and Coinmama are cryptocurrency exchange platforms.

Population: 9,501,451

Business Culture Characteristics: Business meetings tend to be low-key but formal, personal relationships.

Literacy: 99.9%

Economy: Public debt, fragile private sector.
GDP: $27,700

Bhutan

Cryptocurrencies: Krake, Robinhood, Coinbase, Binance, Gemini, Bybit, MEXc, Bitstamp, and OKX
Population: 884,546
Business Culture Characteristics: Politeness, punctuality
Literacy: 66.6%
Economy: Hydropower, services, agriculture
GDP: $14,000

Brazil

Regulation: cryptocurrency accepted.

Cryptocurrency: Mostly legal investment. Binance and Foxbit are the exchange platforms.

Population: 220,051,512

Business Culture Characteristics: It is characterized by openness, patience, and flexibility. The Brazilian culture is one of the world's most varied and diverse cultures. It is derived from influences from Portuguese, African, indigenous, and other European cultures. The family structure and values are very important in Brazil, with large, extended families being the norm. Brazilians tend to be affectionate, tactile people with a smaller sense of personal space.

There is a level of informality in how Brazilians greet and address each other. Shaking hands, hugs, and kisses on the cheek are common greetings though women tend to touch more and greet with kisses. Brazilians usually address teachers, doctors, priests, and other professionals using their titles followed by their names. Body language and terms of address also vary with an individual's social standing.

Brazilian culture has class distinctions based on one's socioeconomic status and ethnic background. Brazil's business community is highly educated, and a significant portion of the population is well-versed in English as well as another foreign language. The expectation when conducting business in Brazil is to deal with the individual first, not the business. A relationship will need to be established, as Brazilians prefer to take their time to get to know one another before committing to a contract. Punctuality at events and dinners is expected. In addition, formal dress is the norm within the business setting. When in doubt, it is considered better to overdress than to appear too casual in appearance.

Literacy: 94.7%

Economy: Industrial-led economy

GDP per capita: $18,600

Bulgaria

Regulation: Mostly legal investment

Cryptocurrency: Cryptocurrency exchange platforms are Bybit, Binance, Uphold, BitStamp, and Crypto.com

Population: 6,782,659

Business Culture Characteristics: Based on relationships, trust, and business etiquette.

Literacy: 98.4%

Economy: Upper-middle income

GDP: $33,300

Bolivia

Regulation: Banned

Cryptocurrency: Banned

Population: 12,311,974

Business Culture Characteristics: The Bolivian government is eager to attract foreign investment. Most members of Bolivia's private sector are experienced businesspersons with ample direct exposure to the United States and West European customs and procedures.

Very formal. Treat those in authority with particular respect. Spend time cultivating relationships.

Literacy: 93.8%

Economy: Resources are rich economies.

GDP: $9,700

Cayman Islands

Regulation: Virtual assets are accepted.

Cryptocurrency: Cryptocurrency exchange platforms are Roboforex, AvaTrade, FPmarkets, XTB Trading, Pepperstone, and eToro.

Population: 66,653

Business Culture Characteristics: Influence by Afro-Caribbeans.

Literacy: 98.7%

Economy: Dominant offshore banking

GDP: $79,600

China

Regulations: This does not recognize cryptocurrencies as legal tender.

Cryptocurrency: The country has its own form of digital currency called the e-yuan, which has many million users. Cryptocurrency exchange platforms are OKX, Huobi, Binance, BitFinex, Gate.io, BTCC, CoinEgg, and ZB.com

Population: 1,416,043,270

Business Culture Characteristics: The Chinese give a lot of importance to the value of time and most meetings commence on time. They place a lot of emphasis on precision and detail when designing contracts. They pay close attention to long-standing relationships because it is believed that the culture of each business is better understood by building long-term relationships. It does take a significant amount of time for a business entering China to understand the legal aspects as well as the culture of negotiating deals.

In establishing business deals, the business that invests in understanding and appreciating the Chinese culture succeeds. On the other side, the Chinese understand the cultural differences and would not expect foreigners to get fully acclimatized to their traditions. They would go with their assessment of their partners rather than the custom alignment. In order to prevent loss face, most Chinese would prefer to work on a one-on-one basis with the party and not through an intermediary.

In terms of nonverbal communication, it would help to assess the status of the officials who have convened to discuss the contract.

Most Chinese meetings are developed to pleasantries in order to wait for the most opportunities moment to discuss formal aspects of the contract or the business. Most Chinese tend to become rigid in posture when their position is in jeopardy.

Literacy: 96.8%

Economy: One of the world's top two economies, manufacturing, and exporting.

GDP per capita: $22,100

Colombia

Regulation: Not yet regulated

Cryptocurrency: Cryptocurrency exchange platforms are Bybit, eToro, Binance, and Gate.io.

Population: 49,588,357

Business Culture Characteristics: Tends to be quite formal. Prefer doing business in person.

Literacy: 96%

Economy: Consistent growth

GDP: $18,800

Canada

Regulations: Mostly legal investment. Bitcoin is considered a commodity for income tax purposes by the Canada Revenue Agency. Any income that a Canadian receives from a cryptocurrency sale or exchange must be reported as business income or a capital gain. Cryptocurrency exchanges are considered money service businesses and must be registered with the Financial Transactions and Report Analysis Centre of Canada.

Cryptocurrency: Cryptocurrency is accepted. Cryptocurrency exchange platforms are Bitbuy, VirgoCX, Wealthsimple, Crypto, Netcoins, Newton, Coinsmart, and Coinbase.

Population: 38,794,813

Business Culture Characteristics: Canadians are formal as compared to the Americans. The culture in Canada is so markedly influenced by European norms that it becomes imperative for businesspeople to address the region separately. Diversity, cultural differences, conservative, politeness, respect.

Literacy: 99%

Economy: One of the world's largest economies, US trade partner.

GDP: $55,800

Costa Rica

Regulation: Mostly legal investment

Cryptocurrency: Legal; Cryptocurrency exchange platforms are eToro, Skilling, and Binance.

Population: 5,265,575

Business Culture Characteristics: Building relationships and trust are crucial. Flexibility and patience are important. Dress smartly.

Literacy: 98%

Economy: Trade-based upper-middle income

GDP: $25,800

Cuba

Regulation: The Central bank issues regulations for digital asset service providers.

Cryptocurrency: The Central bank recognizes Bitcoin.

Population: 10,985,974

Business Culture Characteristics: They work around regularity restrictions.

Literacy: 99.7%

Economy: State-run planned economy

GDP: $12,300

Cambodia

Regulation: No regulating framework.

Cryptocurrency: Legal. Cryptocurrency exchange platforms are Binance, Kraken, and Coinmama.

Population: 17,063,669

Business Culture Characteristics: Conservative, formal dress, punctuality, harmony, seniority.

Literacy: 84%
Economy: One of the fastest-growing economies, Tourism
GDP: $5,100

Chile

Regulation: Mostly legal investment.

Cryptocurrency: Cryptocurrency exchange platforms are Binance, Krake, and eToro.

Population: 18,664,652

Business Culture Characteristics: Formal and conservative appearance is important. Business structures are hierarchical, and decision-making is made at the top.

Literacy: 97%
Economy: Export-driven, leader in copper
GDP: $29,500

Cyprus

Regulation: Mostly legal investment.

Cryptocurrency: Cryptocurrency is accepted. Cryptocurrency exchange platforms are eToro, Kraken, Uphold, OKX, and KuCoin.

Population: 1,320,525

Business Culture Characteristics: Punctuality, trust, personal relationships.

Literacy: 99.4%
Economy: Service-based, high income
GDP: $50,600

Czechoslovakia [Czech Republic]

Regulation: Mostly legal investment.

Cryptocurrency: Cryptocurrency exchange platforms are Binance, Kraken, and Bitpanda.

Population: 10,503,734

Business Culture Characteristics: Business is conducted slowly and hierarchically.

Literacy: 99%

Economy: High income, diversified.
GDP: $50,961

Denmark

Regulation: Mostly legal investment.

Cryptocurrency: Cryptocurrency exchange platforms are Bybit, Capital, Binance, Plus500, Bitpanda, Uphold, and Arabase.

Population: 5,973,136

Business Culture Characteristics: Teamwork, open communication, flexible business hours

Literacy: 99%

Economy: Diversified EU trade-based economy.

GDP: $72,000

Dominica

Regulation: Yet to enact laws governing cryptocurrencies.

Cryptocurrency: Cryptocurrency transactions in Dominica are impossible to hack as these are specialized encryption techniques.

Population: 74,661

Business Culture Characteristics: Dealings are formal. Punctuality is expected.

Literacy: 93.7%

Economy: Emerging ecotourism.

GDP per capita: $16,000

Ecuador

Regulation: Cryptocurrency is not a means of payment.

Cryptocurrency: Transaction takes place in a fully decentralized market.

Population: 18,309,984

Business Culture Characteristics: Spending time cultivating relationships.

Literacy: 93.6%

Economy: Major banana exporter

GDP: $14,300

El Salvador

Regulation: No legal framework

Cryptocurrency: Cryptocurrency is the official legal currency. They adopted Bitcoin as their currency in 2021. They believe that Bitcoin is the path to financial freedom. Binance, Kraken, and Gemini. El Salvador holds $350 million [approximately]. Bitcoin is what public government holds. Average price is $59,358.

Population: 6,628,702

Business Culture Characteristics: Business is conducted after a relationship has been established.

Literacy: 90%

Economy: Service-based economy

GDP: $11,300

Estonia

Regulations: Mostly legal investment.

Cryptocurrency: They have embraced blockchain technology. Estonia has digital ID cards for online services and was the first country to offer e-Residency, a digital identity, available to anyone in the world interested in operating a business online. Binance, Kraken, Bitpanda are cryptocurrency exchange platforms.

Population: 1,193,791

Business Culture Characteristics: Characterized by individualism, patriotism, and strong work ethics.

Literacy: 99.9%

GDP: $ 42,000

Finland

Regulation: Mostly legal investment.

Cryptocurrency: Cryptocurrency exchange platforms are Binance, Kraken, and Bitpanda

Population: 5,626,414

Business Culture Characteristics: Informal work relationships, open communications, trust, mutual respect, and punctuality.

Literacy: 100%

Economy: Highly industrialized, export-based
GDP: $57,500

France

Regulation: Mostly legal investment.

Cryptocurrency: Cryptocurrency exchange platforms are Binance, Kraken, and Bitpanda.

Population: 68,374,591

Business Culture Characteristics: Business communication is formal and respectful; Greetings with handshakes, using titles, punctuality, and exchange of business cards.

Literacy: 99%

Economy: High income, advanced, and diversified EU economy.

GDP: $55,200

Germany

Regulation: Mostly legal investment.

Cryptocurrency: Binance, Kraken, and Bitpanda are the cryptocurrency exchange platforms.

Population: 84,119,100

Business Culture Characteristics: German managers are experts in their fields and expected to lead others by exhibiting strong and clear leadership skills. Their concept of business dealings involves formal interaction with the clientele where it would be advantageous to the client to be well prepared for the meeting, as Germans generally come well prepared for their meetings. The individual never mentions his/her achievements or offers insight into his/her personal matters. In Germany, it is important that the dealings are made specific, either in writing or verbally. This is specifically because Germans pay attention to detail, and anything that is not specified will be considered in breach of trust.

Germans tend to prefer the formal form of addressing people, and the use of first names should be avoided. For the Germans, greeting is almost always a firm handshake. There is significant emphasis placed on the seniority of one employee over another, and this inadvertently also relates to the formality of relationships within the company. Privacy, punctuality, hierarchy, loyalty, professionalism, reliability, and business cards are exchanged.

Literacy: 99%

Economy: Leading EU economy, service-based

GDP: $61,900

Greece

Regulation: Mostly legal investment.

Cryptocurrency: Cryptocurrency exchange platforms are Binance, Kraken, and Bitpanda.

Population: 10,461,091

Business Culture Characteristics: Hierarchical structure

Literacy: 97.9%

Economy: Tourism and shipping

GDP: $36,300

Grenada

Regulation: Does not have any specific legislation to regulate cryptocurrencies.

Cryptocurrency: Binance and Kraken are the cryptocurrency exchange platforms.

Population: 114,621

Business culture Characteristics: They are serious about their jobs.

Literacy: 98.6%

Economy: Tourism.

GDP per capita: $16,000

Guatemala

Regulation: Yet to be legalizing cryptocurrency

Cryptocurrency:

Population: 18,255,216

Business Culture Characteristics: Make appointments before visiting; Punctuality; Hierarchical business environment; Persona; Connections for successful business.

Literacy: 83.5%

Economy: Growing Central American economy

GDP: $12,700

Georgia

Regulation: Mostly legal investment.

Cryptocurrency: Cryptocurrency is legal. Cryptocurrency exchange platforms are Binance and Coinmama.

Population: 4,900,961

Business Culture Characteristics: Business meetings tend to be relatively relaxed affairs.

Literacy: 99.6%

Economy: Transportation and construction

GDP: $22,200

Ghana

Cryptocurrency: Binance, Kraken, and Gemini

Population: 34,589,092

Business Culture Characteristics: Hierarchical structure, formal, courteous, relationships.

Literacy: 58%

Economy: Lower-middle income

GDP: $ 6,700

Hongkong

Regulation: Mostly legal investment.

Cryptocurrency: Cryptocurrency exchange platforms are Binance, Coinmama, and Huobi

Population: 7,297,821

Business Culture Characteristics: Exchange business cards, long-term business relationships, hierarchical structure, and dress codes.

Literacy: 97%

Economy: High-income, tourism, and service-based economy

GDP per capita: $64,400

Honduras

Regulation: Yet to create a regulatory framework

Cryptocurrency: Cryptocurrency exchange platforms are Binance, Krake, and Coinmama.

Population: 9,571,352

Business Culture Characteristics: Business negotiations tend to be slower. More emphasis on relationships.

Literacy: 88.5%

Economy: Second fastest-growing Central American economy

GDP: $6,500

Hungary

Cryptocurrency: eTORO, Bybit, Uphold, Binance, and Kraken.

Population: 9,855,745

Business Culture Characteristics: Relationships, Direct eye contact

Literacy: 99%

Economy: High-income

GDP: $40,600

India

Regulation: Mostly legal investment.

Cryptocurrency: Cryptocurrency exchange platforms are WazirX, Binance, Coinbase, Coinmama, and Unocoin.

Population 1,409,128,296

Business Culture Characteristics Conducting business in India requires considering certain cultural aspects and nuances. The use of the first name for address should be avoided. The usual method used will be to press one's palms together in front of the chest and say "Namaste," meaning "Greetings to you." The attitude toward women is one of respect, and the distance between men and women is one that should be maintained when addressing them.

In conducting business, it would be appropriate to chart the dimensions of the contractual agreement in order to have a document to refer to over an extended period of time. Diversity, privacy, punctuality, and physical presence are essential.

Literacy: 74.4%
Economy: Largest South Asian economy.
GDP per capita: $9,200

Indonesia

Regulation: Mostly legal investment.

Cryptocurrency: Tadpole, Xaurius, BotXCoin, Meong, Toko Token, and Zipmex Token are the cryptocurrency exchange platforms.

Population: 281,562,465

Business Culture Characteristics: Diversity of people, family-oriented, high value on social harmony, hierarchical.

Literacy: 96%

Economy: One of the fastest-growing economies, upper-middle income

GDP per capita: $14,100

Iran

Regulation: Mostly legal investment.

Cryptocurrency: International payments are allowed. Cryptocurrency exchange platforms are Nobitex, Wallex.ir, Excoino, Aban Tether, and Bit24.cash

Population: 88,386,937

Business Culture Characteristics: Meeting punctuality, business relationships.

Literacy: 88.7%

Economy: State-controlled economy

GDP: $16,200

Ireland

Cryptocurrency: eTORO, Kraken, Uphold, Revolut, Crypto.com, Coinbase, and Binance.

Population: 5,233,461

Business Culture Characteristics: Punctuality, relaxed meeting

Literacy: 99%

Economy: Export based

GDP: $115, 600

Israel

Cryptocurrency: CoinSmart, GEMINI, and eTORO

Population: 9,402,617

Business Culture Characteristics: Informal, straightforward, entrepreneurial.

Literacy: 97.8%

Economy: High income, technology & industrial-based economy.

GDP: $48,300

Italy

Regulation: Mostly legal investment.

Cryptocurrency: Binance, Kraken, and Bitpanda are the cryptocurrency exchange platforms.

Population: 60,964,931

Business Culture Characteristics: Casual workplace relations, hierarchical.

Literacy: 99.2%

Economy: Core EU economy, strong services, manufacturing, tourism

GDP: $52,700

Iceland

Regulation: Mostly legal investment

Cryptocurrency: Legal. Cryptocurrency exchange platforms are Binance, Krake, and Bitpanda

Population: 364,036

Business Culture Characteristics: Everyone is treated equally, friendliness, personal relationships.

Literacy: 99%

Economy: High-income

GDP: $66,500

Jamaica

Cryptocurrency: Binance, Kraken, Gemini

Population: 2,823,713

Business Culture Characteristics: Respect, politeness, punctuality.
Literacy: 89%
Economy: Upper-middle income
GDP: $10,300

Japan

Regulation: Mostly legal investment.

Cryptocurrency: Cryptocurrency is accepted. Cryptocurrency exchange platforms are Binance, bitFlyer, and Coincheck.

Population: 123,201,945

Business Culture Characteristics: The Japanese get familiar with the culture of the people whom they deal with. Japanese are very polite and try to accommodate everybody's needs and wishes. When approaching the Japanese, one should take caution in not being too direct because this would mean that if they are not able to answer or accommodate, they query. That would result in them losing face in front of the foreign party.

Given the level of collectivism in Japanese society, it translates to such a system in the workplace. Most executives convene as a group, and often it is difficult to determine who is at the top of the hierarchy. Politeness, sensitivity, and good manners form the foundation of businesses in Japan. Being loyal to a business is considered a virtue, and many executives spend a number of years with the business. This translates to a long-term relationship with partners in business scenarios.

Significant emphasis is placed on the actual interaction with the clients. The Japanese tend to be very formal in their meetings. Time is sacrosanct in Japan, and they would like to be aware of any delays in advance. They prefer formal dress in client meetings and give a lot of importance to business cards. Business cards need to be exchanged during meetings. Accept business cards with respect and keep them safe, as forgetting to pick up their business cards is considered impolite and is considered a proxy for the lack of interest in a long-term relationship.

Literacy: 99%

Economy: Fourth largest trade-oriented economy
GDP per capita: $46,300

Jordan

Cryptocurrency: Binance, Kraken, and PKX
Population: 11,174,024
Business Culture Characteristics: Conservative, hierarchical structure.
Literacy: 98.4%
Economy: Upper-middle income
GDP: $9, 400

Kazakhstan

Cryptocurrency: Binance, Kraken, OKX, Bybit, Gate.io, and MEXC
Population: 20,260,006
Business Culture Characteristics: Handshake.
Literacy: 99.8%
Economy: Oil and Gas
GDP: $35, 500

North Korea

Cryptocurrency: N/A
Population: 26,298,666
Business Culture Characteristics:
Literacy: 100%
Economy: Centrally planned economy
GDP: $1, 700

South Korea

Cryptocurrency: Upbit, BitHumb, Coinone, and KorBit
Population: 52,081,799
Business Culture Characteristics: Hierarchical structure, strong work ethics.
Literacy: 99%

Economy: Export and technology-oriented
GDP: $50, 600

Kenya

Regulation: Mostly legal investment.

Cryptocurrency: They have the mobile payment system—M-PESA which is used by 90% of all Kenyans—to illustrate that digital banking is possible with high rates of poverty and relatively poor infrastructure. Cryptocurrency exchange platforms are Avatrade, FXGT, FBS, TickMill, JustMarkets, and FxPro.

Population: 58,246,378

Business Culture Characteristics: Informal, open, shaking hands, exchanging business cards.

Literacy: 82.6%

Economy: Third-largest sub-Saharan economy. Strong agriculture, emerging services, and tourism industries.

GDP per capita: $5,700

Laos

Cryptocurrency: Binance, Kraken, and OKX
Population: 7,953,556
Business Culture Characteristics: Punctuality.
Literacy: 84.7%
Economy: Lower-middle income
GDP: $8, 400

Latvia

Cryptocurrency: Coinbase, Binance, and Bitpanda

Population: 1,801,246

Business Culture Characteristics: Punctuality, dress code, direct communication.

Literacy: 99.8%

Economy: High-income

GDP: $37, 800

Lithuania

Regulation: Mostly legal investment.

Cryptocurrency: eToro, Uphold, OKX, Bbit, and Bitpanda are the cryptocurrency exchange platforms.

Population: 2,628,186

Business Culture Characteristics: Characterized by business communications, and business etiquette.

Literacy: 99.8%

Economy: High income

GDP: $46,200

Luxembourg

Regulation: Mostly legal investment.

Cryptocurrency: Cryptocurrency exchange platforms are eToro, BitStamp, Binance, and Uphold.

Population: 671,254

Business Culture Characteristics: Punctuality and politeness.

Literacy: 100%

Economy: High income

GDP: $132,400

Mexico

Regulation: Mostly legal investment.

Cryptocurrency: Cryptocurrencies are considered as commodities. Cryptocurrency exchange platforms are Bybit, Kraken, and Gate.io.

Population: 130,739,927

Business Culture Characteristics: The Mexicans are seen to be a hospitable and warm group of people. Mexican attitude and behavior tend to be a combination of both European and Native American influences. To the Mexican, the uniqueness of the individual should be recognized. The family plays a chief role in an average Mexican's life, and emphasis is placed on knowing one's family ties and connections prior to conducting business with them. Family relationships tend to be the basis upon which bonds are established and fostered.

It is necessary for the foreign business to understand that questions posed regarding family are a means of ascertaining their well-being rather than an intrusion into privacy. Most Mexicans speak in a circulatory manner and often avoid any direct references or conversation. In order to ensure that there is a pleasant atmosphere, Mexicans will tell their counterparts what they would want to hear, rather than mention anything harsh. This is not to say that they knowingly flatter in order to get their work done. The purpose is often to please the other party and to make them feel at home.

When approaching the organizational structure, it is important to note the hierarchy within the business. The top-down system is very much in effect, and seniority is considered to be a discriminating factor between levels. It is advisable for the foreign concern to be aware of the ranking of officials and alter its decision-making style based on hierarchical differentiation. One major aspect to note is machismo—the concept of masculinity that infiltrates into business dealings as well. Though women are represented in several managerial positions, it is believed that only a man should earn the respect of society and demonstrate leadership qualities.

Literary: 95.2%

Economy: One of the largest economies, manufacturing sector.

GDP: $22,400

Mauritius

Regulation: Mostly legal investment.

Cryptocurrency: Binance, Kraken, and Coinmama are the cryptocurrency exchange platforms.

Population: 1,310,504

Business Culture Characteristics: Punctual to meetings, shaking hands, and exchanging business cards.

Literacy: 92.2%

Economy: Upper-middle income

GDP: $26,600

Malta

Regulations: Mostly legal investment.

Cryptocurrency: They embrace blockchain technology. They support international blockchain and cryptocurrency-related companies. Cryptocurrency exchange platforms are eToro, Uphold, Bybit, and OKX.

Population: 469,300

Business Culture Characteristics: Business communications and business etiquette.

Literacy: 94.9%

Economy: High income.

GDP: $57,200

Malaysia

Regulation: Mostly legal investment.

Cryptocurrency: Binance, Kraken, and Coinmama are the cryptocurrency exchange platforms.

Population: 34,564,810

Business Culture Characteristics: Hierarchical, teamwork, collaborations.

Literacy: 95%

Economy: Upper-middle income, high-labor productivity.

GDP per capita: $33,600

Morocco

Regulation: Mostly legal investment.

Cryptocurrency: Cryptocurrency exchange platforms are Bybit, Kraken, OKX, Gate.io, and KuCoin

Population: 37,387,585

Business Culture Characteristics: Hierarchical, interpersonal relationships.

Literacy: 75.9%

Economy: Lower-middle income, tourism.

GDP: $8,800

Montserrat

Regulation: Yet to enact laws governing cryptocurrencies.

Cryptocurrency: *Skilling* is the cryptocurrency exchange.

Population: 5,468

Business Culture Characteristics: The people are usually friendly and relaxed.

Literacy: 97%

Economy: High-income economy, geothermal, and solar power.

GDP per capita: $34,000

Mongolia

Regulation: Mostly legal investment.

Cryptocurrency: Legal. Cryptocurrency exchange platforms are Binance, Kraken, and Coinmama.

Population: 3,281,676

Business Culture Characteristics: Generous hosts.

Literacy: 99.2%

Economy: Lower-middle income

GDP: $16,300

Nicaragua

Cryptocurrency: Binance, Kraken, and OKX

Population: 6,676,948

Business Culture Characteristics: Negotiations.

Literacy: 82.6%

Economy: Low-income

GDP: $7, 300

Norway

Regulation: Mostly legal investment.

Cryptocurrency: The cryptocurrency exchange platforms are Binance, Kraken, and Bitpanda.

Population: 5,509,73

Business Culture Characteristics: Non-hierarchical, quite informal, values independence.

Literacy: 100%

Economy: High-income; Large state-owned energy companies.
GDP: $90,500

Nigeria

Regulation: Mostly legal investment.

Cryptocurrency: Cryptocurrency exchange platforms are Binance, Luno, Quidax, NairaEx, Kraken, Coinbase, Bybit, and KuCoin.

Population: 236,747,130

Business Culture Characteristics: Personal relationships, adaptability, flexibility, and patience.

Literacy: 62%

Economy: Larger African Market economy, Major oil exporter.

GDP: $5,700

Nepal

Regulation: Banned transaction

Cryptocurrency: Illegal. Cryptocurrency exchange platforms are Binance, Skilling, and Avatrade.

Population: 31,122,387

Business Culture Characteristics: Handshake

Literacy: 71.2%

Economy: Low-income

GDP: $4,700

Netherlands

Regulation: Mostly legal investment.

Cryptocurrency: Cryptocurrency exchange platforms are eToro, crypto.com, BitStamp, Coinbase, Bitvaro, and LiteBit.

Population: 17,772,378

Business Culture Characteristics: Business communications, hierarchical.

Literacy: 99%

Economy: High income

GDP: $69,300

Oman

Cryptocurrency: Rain, BitOasis, Paybis, and Bitcoin ATMS

Population: 3,901,992

Business Culture Characteristics: Personal relationships, respect, face-to-face communications, hierarchical structure.

Literacy: 98.6%

Economy: High-income, oil-based

GDP: $40, 000

Panama

Cryptocurrency: Bybit, Binance, Kraken, Coinbase, and BingX

Population: 4,470,241

Business Culture Characteristics: Hierarchical, relationships.

Literacy: 95.7%

Economy: Upper-middle income

GDP: $35, 800

Peru

Regulation: Mostly legal investment.

Cryptocurrency: Binance, Kraken, and Coinmama are the exchange platforms for cryptocurrencies.

Population: 32,600,249

Business Culture Characteristics: Hierarchical with decision-making done from the top.

Literacy: 94.5%

Economy: Upper-middle income

GDP: $15,100

Paraguay

Regulation: No regulatory framework.

Cryptocurrency: Cryptocurrency exchange platforms are Binance, Kraken, and Coinmama.

Population: 7,552,549

Business Culture Characteristics: Generally conservative. Cleanliness is expected.

Literacy: 95%

Economy: Upper-middle-income South American economy
GDP: $15,700

Philippines

Regulation: Mostly legal investment.

Cryptocurrency: Binance, OKX, and Kraken are the cryptocurrency exchange platforms.

Population: 118,277,063

Business Culture Characteristics: Trust, loyalty, conservative approach to decision-making.

Literacy: 96.3%

Economy: Diversified economy, shipbuilding

GDP per capita: $9,700

Pakistan

Regulation: Mostly legal investment.

Cryptocurrency: Cryptocurrency exchange platforms are WazirX, Binance, Coinbase, Coinmama, and Unocoin.

Population: 252,363,571

Business Culture Characteristics: It is good to arrive on time; wait to be introduced; and exchange business cards.

Literacy: 58%

Economy: Lower-middle income

GDP: $5,600

Poland

Cryptocurrency: eTORO, Bybit, Gate.io, Binance, Rucoin, Bitget, HTX, and OKX

Population: 38,746,310

Business Culture Characteristics: Hierarchical, respect authority, formal communication, personal relationships.

Literacy: 99.7%

Economy: High-income

GDP: $44, 100

Portugal

Regulation: Mostly legal investment.

Cryptocurrency: Cryptocurrency exchange platforms are Uphold, Bitpanda, Bybit, eToro, and Binance.

Population: 10,207,177

Business Culture Characteristics: Characterized by a strong emphasis on building relationships, hierarchical structure punctuality.

Literacy: 95.9%

Economy: High-income, tourism

GDP: $41,700

Qatar

Cryptocurrency: Rain, eTORO, Bybit, OKX, and Gate.io

Population: 2,552,088

Business Culture Characteristics: Hierarchical, personal relationships, dress codes.

Literacy: 93.4%

Economy: High-income, oil and gas

GDP: $113, 200

Romania

Cryptocurrency: eTORO, Bybit, Uphold, Kraken, OKX, MEXC, Binance, Bitpanda, Kucoin, and UTX

Population: 18,148,155

Business Culture Characteristics: Punctuality, Formal, dress codes.

Literacy: 98.8%

Economy: High-income

GDP: $40, 500

Russia

Regulation: Digital currencies cannot be used to pay for any goods and services.

Cryptocurrency: Cryptocurrency exchange platforms are Bybit, Binance, Gate.io, OKX, and KuCoin.

Population: 140,820,810

Business Culture Characteristics: Characterized by caution, persistence, and strong hierarchy which modestly causes a certain bureaucracy to occur.

Literacy: 99.7%

Economy: Natural resources, energy exporters, oil and gas exporters.

GDP: $39,800

Senegal

Cryptocurrency: Binance, Kraken, and OKX

Population: 18,847,519

Business Culture Characteristics: Team spirit, loyalty.

Literacy: 56.3%

Economy: Low-middle income

GDP: $4,400

Saint Kitts and Nevis

Regulation: Mostly legal investment.

Cryptocurrency: There is a legal framework for cryptocurrencies that will ensure that each provider participating in cryptocurrency services must register with the government.

Population: 55,133

Business Culture Characteristics: Material possessions are important. Education matters greatly.

Literacy: 98%

Economy: High-income, tourism-based economy. Growing offshore financial and telecommunications hub.

GDP per capita: $31,000

Saint Vincent and the Grenadines

Regulation: The government has not passed any legislation.

Cryptocurrency: They are participating in implementing cryptocurrency as a fiat currency.

Population: 100,804

Business Culture Characteristics: Easygoing people. Informal and relaxed lifestyle.

Literacy: 96%

Economy: Upper-middle-income economy, agriculture, and tourism.

GDP per capita: $18,000

Saint Lucia

Regulation: Yet to enact laws governing cryptocurrencies.

Cryptocurrency: Cryptocurrency transactions in Dominica are impossible to hack as these are specialized encryption techniques.

Population: 168,038

Business Culture Characteristics: Influenced by African, East Indian, French, and English heritage.

Literacy: 90%

Economy: Tourism-based economy

GDP per capita: $23,000

Saudi Arabia

Regulation: Mostly legal investment.

Cryptocurrency: Cryptocurrency exchange platforms are Binance, Bybit, Rain, OKX, and Gate.io.

Population: 36,544,431

Business Culture Characteristics: The majority of the population in Saudi Arabia is native to the country, with foreigners from the Middle East, Africa, and other countries comprising the remainder. Most of the population, including the traditionally nomadic population, has settled in the major cities throughout the country. One-fourth of the population originates from the Bedouin people, the majority of the nomadic population in the region, who hold a prominent position in the society.

Saudi Arabia, as defined by Saudi Law, is a Muslim nation, with Islam being the only recognized religion. The majority of residents, about 90%, are Sunni Muslims who follow the Salafism Islamic code, and 5% of the population are Shia Muslims. Beyond the stereotyping that all Arabs are Muslims, what is essential to note is that the religion complements the Arab way of life. Arab means pertaining to Arabia and carries with it the cultural connotation and not the religious association.

Saudi Arabians tend to perceive business to be a means to gain an understanding of the Middle Eastern methods of management. Time is a major commodity, but patience is a virtue. It is beneficial for the foreign party to spend time getting accustomed to Arab culture. Arabs are considered to be people of great emotional depth who believe in expressing their loyalty and friendship as key to an ongoing relationship.

In conducting business, they tend to be warm and hospitable and, when the party becomes more aware of the nuances of the culture, make it a very easygoing discussion. The concept of the individual is very important in Arab culture. One cannot afford to lose face or ruin his family's name in the process of dealing with others. There is a hierarchy in society, whether stipulated or otherwise, and an individual who has been shamed loses his status in the eyes of the group. Negotiating is considered to be part of the average business deal, and one should ideally expect that it will take time for a unanimous decision to be reached.

Literacy: 97.6%

Economy: High income, oil-based economy.

GDP per capita: $49,600

Spain

Regulation: Mostly egal investment.

Cryptocurrency: Binance, Kraken, and Bitpanda are the cryptocurrency exchange platforms.

Population: 47,280,433

Business Culture Characteristics: Hierarchical; appointments are important; business cards are exchanged.

Literacy: 98.6%

Economy: High income

GDP: $46,400

Singapore

Regulations: Mostly legal investment.

Cryptocurrency: Singapore's Central Bank launched a project to use blockchain technology for its interbank payments. Singapore has a modern digital identity system that could easily be connected to a blockchain. They have a digital identity to IoT sensors that optimize public records. Cryptocurrency exchange platforms are Phemex, Binance, BYDFi, PrimeXBT, Coinbase, and BingX.

Population: 6,028,459

Business Culture Characteristics: Relationship-oriented, hierarchical, negotiations at a slow pace, require trust and loyalty, observe etiquette.

Literacy: 97.5%

Economy: High-income

GDP: $127,500

Slovenia

Regulation: Mostly legal investment.

Cryptocurrency: Cryptocurrency exchange platforms are Bitget, Binance, KuCoin, eToro, and Bybit.

Population: 2,097,893

Business Culture Characteristics: Hierarchical, patience, respect in business communications, business meetings are conducted slowly.

Literacy: 99.7%

Economy: High income

GDP: $48,100

South Korea

Regulation: Mostly legal investment.

Cryptocurrency: Binance, Korbit, and Upbit are cryptocurrency exchange platforms.

Population: 52,081,799

Business Culture Characteristics: Values respect, hierarchy, business cards exchanged.

Literacy: 98.8%

Economy: Strong export-driven, global healthcare technology, automobile manufacturing.

GDP per capita: $50,600

Sweden

Regulation: Mostly legal investment.

Cryptocurrency: Cryptocurrency exchange platforms are Binance, Kraken, and Bitpanda are the cryptocurrency exchange platforms.

Population: 10,589,835

Business Culture Characteristics: Based on egalitarianism, professionalism, punctuality, and work-life balance.

Literacy: 99%

Economy: Small, open, competitive & thriving economy.

GDP: $64,200

Switzerland

Regulation: Mostly legal investment.

Cryptocurrency: Binance, OKX, and Kraken are the cryptocurrency exchange platforms.

Population: 8,860,574

Business Culture Characteristics: Ease of doing business; Business culture is relaxed and polite. Hierarchical in structure; Quite conservative in terms of values.

Literacy: 99%

Economy: High income, banking and financial hub.

GDP: $82,900

South Africa

Regulation: Mostly legal investment.

Cryptocurrency: Cryptocurrency exchange platforms are Binance, Coinbase, Coinmama, and Kraken.

Population: 60,442,647

Business Culture Characteristics: South Africa is a country with a very diverse culture rich in ethnic and language differences among the population. The majority of the population is comprised of White, Colored, Asian/Indian, and Native African ethnic groups. In terms of language, there are eleven official languages spoken, and these tend to be vernacular or dialects.

Conducting business dealings in South Africa is rather tedious. Most Africans do not stand on formality, and though that connotes a relaxed attitude, they do not fall into that category either. Personal matters are kept separate from business dealings. Similarly, it is considered impolite to discuss business at home. Some of the informality can be seen in the way people are most commonly addressed by their first name in business settings. Also, prefixes such as Mr. and Mrs. and professional titles such as Dr. are not commonly used.

Most business is conducted in English. However, special note must be taken of the accent and undertones of speech. For example, the use of overly diplomatic language by a foreigner may be interpreted as a lack of commitment or dishonesty. As such, it is preferred to speak plainly and directly in many instances. It is also preferred that hard selling is not used as a tactic. Such behavior would be perceived negatively. Instead, a friendlier approach that focuses on the relationship would allow for better negotiations. In terms of gestures, handshaking, and backslapping are the norm for greeting or doing an introduction. South Africa is a conservative society, and dress should be formal and appropriate for the occasion, particularly in business settings.

Literacy: 95%
Economy: Upper-middle income
GDP: $14,300

Trinidad and Tobago

Cryptocurrency: Binance, Kraken, and OKX
Population: 1,408,966
Business Culture Characteristics: Respect, dignity.
Literacy: 99%
Economy: High-income
GDP: $28, 500

Turkey

Regulation: Mostly legal investment.

Cryptocurrency: Binance, OKX, and Kraken are the cryptocurrency exchange platforms.

Population: 84,119,531

Business Culture Characteristics: Friendly and sincere, value personal relationships, loyal to business, negotiating takes time—be patient.

Literacy: 96.7%

Economy: Upper-middle income

GDP per capita: $34,400

Tunisia

Regulation: Cryptocurrency banned

Cryptocurrency: not recognized

Population: 12,048,847

Business Culture Characteristics: Personal relationships, trust, hierarchy.

Literacy: 82.7%

Economy: Lower-middle income

GDP: $12,300

Taiwan

Regulation: Mostly legal investment.

Cryptocurrency: Cryptocurrency exchange platforms are Binance, Kraken, and Huobi.

Population: 23,595,274

Business Culture Characteristics: Hierarchical structure, respect for authority, ranks and status, harmony.

Literacy: 98.5%

Economy: Higher income and technology

GDP per capita: $47,800

The Bahamas

Regulation: Mostly legal investment.

Cryptocurrency: Cryptocurrency accepted. Cryptocurrency exchange platforms are Binance, Kraken, and Coinmama

Population: 410,862

Business Culture Characteristics: Punctuality in business meetings & formal attire.

Literacy: 95%

Economy: High-income tourism and financial services economy.

GDP per capita: $32,000

Tanzania

Regulation: Restricted

Cryptocurrency: Not legal. Cryptocurrency exchange platforms are Binance, Kraken, and Coinmama.

Population: 67,462,121

Business Culture Characteristics: Friendly and easygoing. Punctuality is expected.

Literacy: 81.8%

Economy: Emerging low-middle income

GDP: $3,600

Thailand

Regulation: Mostly legal investment.

Cryptocurrency: Bitkub, SaanG, and Binance are the cryptocurrency exchange platforms.

Population: 69,920,998

Business Culture Characteristics: Personal relationships; Hierarchical; Negotiations may be lengthy; Business decisions are slow; They respect foreigners.

Literacy: 94.1%

Economy: Upper-middle income, electronics, automobile manufacturing

GDP: $21,100

Uruguay

Cryptocurrency: Binance, Bitcoin, Ethereum, Kraken, OKX, and Dogecoin

Population: 3,425,330

Business Culture Characteristics: Handshake, group harmony

Literacy: 98.7%
Economy: High-income, export
GDP: $30, 700

Vietnam

Regulation: Mostly legal investment.

Cryptocurrency: Cryptocurrency exchange platforms are BitcoinVN, VBTC, and Binance.

Population: 105,758,975

Business Culture Characteristics: Schedule meetings in advance; Dress appropriately

Literacy: 95.8%

Economy: Lower-middle income

GDP: $13,700

Venezuela

Regulation: Mostly legal investment.

Cryptocurrency: OnixCoin, DashVenezeula, BolivarCoin, and ArepaCoin are the most popular cryptocurrencies.

Population: 31,250,301

Business Culture Characteristics: Arrive on time for meetings. A standard professional greeting is a handshake.

Venezuela is a country comprised of diverse people often characterized by their outgoing and friendly nature. This can be seen in how they greet each other and their body language. Venezuelans are known to stand in close proximity and to use hand gestures, even touching, when in conversation. Greeting with two kisses to the cheek is common for both men and women, although men only kiss women. Men typically greet each other with a firm handshake and some cases a hug depending upon the status of the person.

Venezuela is a patriarchal society that displays machismo, the notion of masculine superiority. As a result, there are distinct differences between the social expectations and the treatment of men and women in society. The belief in traditional gender roles is still prevalent. However, the ideal of machismo is being confronted as more women continue to join the workforce and North American culture penetrates. Venezuela has a strongly defined socioeconomic class structure that is often divided along gender and ethnicity.

The Venezuelan business style is casual, with most of the addresses being informal. The Venezuelans have a strong sense of independence and do not feel compelled to abide by the rules at all times. Overall, their laid-back attitude translates into the business environment. Patriotism toward their country is what most Venezuelans feel. Drawing up contracts in Venezuela is never a reciprocal situation. Most of them are reluctant to commit things to writing yet would appreciate it greatly if the information that they receive is specified.

Literacy: 97.5%

Economy: Privately owned and state-owned, petroleum

GDP: $7,704

Ukraine

Regulation: Mostly legal investment.

Cryptocurrency: Kuna, Binance, and OKX are the cryptocurrency exchange platforms.

Population: 35,661,826

Business Culture Characteristics: Make appointments well in advance, punctuality, arrive on time, personal relationships, hierarchical.

Literacy: 100%

Economy: Lower-middle income economy, major wheat producer and industrial and energy producer

GDP per capita: $16,200

United States of America

Regulations: Mostly legal investment.

Cryptocurrency: Cryptocurrency exchange platforms are Kraken, eToro, Uphold, BinanceUS, and Coinbase.

Population: 341,963,408

Business Culture Characteristics: There are different segments in the population based on demographic and psychographic parameters. The US has inhabitants with origins from all parts of the world with the majority of the population being of European descent. Hispanics (Latinos) and African Americans (Black) constitute the largest minority population in the country.

In terms of geography, the majority of the population in the US lives in urban areas with many of those being in suburban areas. There are also several regional differences that exist in the US in terms of dialect and colloquial behavior. There are four regions in the US and fifty states with each having its own nuances and social norms.

For almost all cultures, it is important to understand how executives view power and authority. Many US managers are highly individualistic, time-conscious, and goal-oriented people. In most cases, the manager is accountable for all decision-making that they are responsible for. Open dialogue is often welcomed in regard to debate and discussing business matters. In addition, communication can be very direct and to the point in order to move business along.

The primary purpose of communication is to exchange information, facts, and opinions. The establishment of a personal relationship is not as important in US business culture. Instead, forming business relationships is deemed more important. However, the act of networking, or building relationships for future opportunities, is often viewed as a vital component of individual advancement. Meetings tend to be formal, with the aim being to solidify a business deal versus cultivating a personal connection. Although cordial exchanges, politeness, and small talk upon introduction are common, these should be viewed as protocol. Other protocols include adhering to meeting times and deadlines, obeying organization structure and hierarchy, and following business policies.

Literacy: 92%

Economy: Higher income, larger importer and second larger exporter

GDP per capita: $73,600

United Kingdom

Regulation: Mostly legal investment.

Cryptocurrency: Cryptocurrency exchange platforms are OKX, Bybit, Binance, Coinbase, and KuCoin.

Population: 68,459,055

Business Culture Characteristics: Characterized by courtesy, politeness, discipline, punctuality, and ironic humor.

Literacy: 99%

Economy: Higher income and sixth larger importer and second larger exporter

GDP per capita: $54,100

United Arab Emirates (UAE)

Regulations: Mostly legal investment.

Cryptocurrency: Their government documents and systems are on the blockchain. They estimated that its blockchain has the potential to save 25.1 million hours in productivity. They have a Global Blockchain Council (GBC) with seven public-private collaborations, combining the skills, and resources of startups, local businesses, and government departments—health care, the diamond trade, title transfers, business registration, tourism, shipping.

Cryptocurrency exchange platforms are Binance, OKX, Kraken, Bybit, and Gate.io.

Population: 10,032,213

Business Culture Characteristics: Multi-cultural society, hierarchical, social networking, personal relationships.

Literacy: 98.1%

Economy: Oil-driven economy

GDP per capita: $75,600

CHAPTER 12

Knowledge of Decentralized Finance (DeFi)

Decentralization

Decentralization is the process by which the activities of an organization, particularly those regarding planning and decision-making, are distributed or delegated away from a central authoritative location or group and given to smaller factions within it. In short, decentralization is the transfer of power, authority, control, and decision-making away from categorized entities to a larger distributed network.

The decentralized network's goal is to create a trustless system where the level of trust needed between network participants is minimal. Decentralization is crucial to blockchain and cryptocurrency. Users can transfer funds and make payments without going through a financial institution via the Bitcoin network. The blockchain is not owned or operated by a single entity. It is kept decentralized via a network of operations called *miners* who run the network by processing and validating transactions.

Core principles of decentralization are autonomy, transparency, censorship resistance, and privacy are the heart of Bitcoin, Ethereum, and most other public blockchains. These public blockchains operate as open networks. Anyone with an Internet connection can access the network and its ecosystem of applications built on them.

Decentralized Finance (DeFi)

Decentralized finance is an emerging financial technology that challenges the current centralized banking system. It eliminates the fees that banks and other financial companies charge for using their services and promotes the use of peer-to-peer transactions. This is a decentralized financial system more suitable for small/medium businesses in developing countries than a traditional financial banking system with a centralized system with intermediaries or third parties. In the crypto space, DeFi is one of the crucial aspects of creating a completely new independent economic-financial system.

Decentralized finance (DeFi) is a blockchain-based form of finance. The public can obtain financial services without relying on centralized intermediaries. Unlike a bank [centralized bank], DeFi is trustless, that is no central authority to control. The contracts in blockchain technology allow cryptocurrency to exist as a decentralized financial system for the global community. In fact, DeFi is transforming global financial services and replacing the centralized financial system.

Decentralized Finance (DeFi) is also known as *open finance.* It furnishes a broad range of financial services which include *credit, savings,* and/or *insurance* in a decentralized manner. Decentralized finance is built on decentralized blockchains. Decentralized blockchains have decentralized architecture, decentralized governance, and decentralized trust. Decentralized finance relies upon contract blockchains, of which *Ethereum* is widely used.

In essence, DeFi is a collective term from a variety of financial applications in cryptocurrency/*blockchain* geared toward disrupting financial intermediaries. It is a financial system built upon *blockchain* technology, aiming to furnish open and permissionless access to digital currency, decentralized applications, Ethereum, and cryptocurrency assets globally. As DeFi continues to disrupt traditional finance, it presents enormous opportunities for financial inclusion, innovation, and democratization. There are challenges around regulation, security, and scalability. These have to be addressed for sustainable growth in years to come.

There are leading companies in the growing field of Decentralized Finance that would transform the global financial systems—Coinbase Global, IBM, Meta Platform, Canaan, and many others.

Uses of Decentralized Finance (DeFi):

1. A peer-to-peer DeFi transaction is where two parties agree to exchange cryptocurrency for goods or services without a third party involved.
2. In DeFi, peer-to-peer can meet an individual's loan needs, an algorithm would match peers that agree on the lender's terms, and a loan is issued. Payments from peer-to-peer are made via a decentralized application or dAPP and follow the same process in the blockchain.
3. Peer-to-peer financial transactions are one of the core premises behind decentralized finance. In brief, a peer-to-peer decentralized is where two parties agree to execute cryptocurrency for goods or services without a third party involved.
4. Anyone with an Internet connection can access a decentralized finance platform and transactions occur without any geographic restriction.
5. Decentralized finance enables any two parties to directly negotiate interest rates and lend money via a decentralized network.
6. Smart contracts published on a blockchain and records of completed transactions are available for anyone to review but do not reveal your identity.
7. Decentralized finance platform doesn't rely upon any centralized financial institutions and are not subject to adver-

sity or bankruptcy. The decentralized nature of decentralized finance protocols mitigates much of this risk.

Cryptocurrency's Decentralized finance [DeFi] in a nutshell:

Decentralized finance [DeFi] has the potential to furnish financial services to billions of unbanked and underbanked people worldwide, enabling them to access loans/save/invest/ transact globally, fostering economic growth and financial independence. By eliminating intermediaries such as banks, decentralized finance [DeFi] can offer lower fees and faster transactions compared to traditional financial systems, making it more cost-effective and user-friendly. With its open-source nature and permissionless access, decentralized finance [DeFi]can foster the development of innovative financial products and services tailored to specific needs and markets, allowing for increased customization and personalization.

As the decentralized finance [DeFi] ecosystem continues to grow, we can expect increased collaboration and interoperability between different blockchain networks, leading to a more connected and seamless user experience. As decentralized finance [DeFi] gains mainstream attention, regulatory frameworks will likely be developed to furnish clarity and protection for users and investors, further legitimizing the industry and encouraging adoption.

Cryptocurrency's decentralized finance will transform the global financial system in years to come. Cryptocurrency has the potential to promote financial inclusion by making financial services accessible to people worldwide where individuals who don't have banking accounts. With decentralized nature of cryptocurrency will furnish financial services, making it possible for those people to participate in the global financial system. This will eventually promote economic growth in countries around the globe.

We find there is the potential to transform the future of the global financial system in significant ways. Cryptocurrency's decentralized nature, security, and potential for financial innovation make it a transformative force in global finance. In essence, cryptocurrency will play a vital role in the global financial system, and it will play a significant role in transforming the future of the global financial sector.

The most significant development in cryptocurrency is the rise of decentralized finance [DeFi] which is an emerging financial system built on blockchain technology that allows for peer-to-peer transactions without intermediaries such as banks. In brief, decentralized finance [DeFi] has created opportunities for financial innovation and has the potential to challenge the present financial systems around the world.

The future of decentralized finance [DeFi] promises immense opportunities for growth, innovation, and financial inclusion. As it continues to progress, it has the potential to revolutionize the way we access and interact with financial services, ultimately empowering individuals and businesses worldwide.

CHAPTER 13

Knowledge of Central Bank Digital Currency (CBDC)

Central Bank Digital Currency (CBDC)

It is digital-based money issued by a central bank rather than a commercial bank and is also a liability of the central bank and denominated in the sovereign currency, as in the case of physical banknotes and coins. CBDC is a form of central bank electronic money that can be used by households and businesses to make payments. In essence, the main objective of CBDC is to provide consumers and businesses with privacy, transferability, convenience, accessibility, and financial security.

A central bank digital currency is also known as digital fiat currency or digital base money in the financial world. This is issued by a central bank rather than by a commercial bank. It is also a liability of the central bank denominated in the sovereign currency, as is the case with physical banknotes/coins. It is a form of central bank electronic money that can be used by households and businesses to make payments. However, the central bank's *digital* currency is *not* well-defined. In brief, CBDC differs from *virtual currency/ cryptocurrency*.

The following central banks have launched a CBDC, namely:

1. The Central Bank of the Bahamas
2. The Eastern Caribbean Central Bank
3. The Central Bank of Nigeria
4. The Bank of Jamaica
5. People's Bank of China
6. The Reserve Bank of India
7. Bank of Russia
8. Some countries have issued or have considered issuing cryptocurrencies. The countries include Venezuela and the Marshall Islands.

Central bank digital currency has two categories of central bank money, retail and wholesale. Retail bank money is the money people have in their wallets or purses. Wholesale bank money is used by community banks for payment clearance and settlements. Retail central bank digital currency has e-money. This is electronic currency wherein the central bank in effect manages a centralized payment system linked to electronic wallets that reside on prepaid cards, smartphones, or other electronic devices. The other version is an account-based central bank digital currency. In this system, individuals and businesses can access central bank accounts. Here, the central bank manages the payment system with the public. The central digital bank currency payment system with a decentralized verification mechanism is managed by the central bank or its authorized agents through a decentralized mechanism that relies on public consensus.

There are two types of retail CBDC. They differ in how individual users access and use their currency.

1. Token-based retail CBDCs are accessible with private keys, public keys, or both. This method of validation allows users to execute transactions anonymously.
2. Account-based retail CBDC requires digital identification to access an account. Central bank digital currencies are

designed to be similar to cryptocurrencies, but they may not require blockchain technology or consensus mechanisms.

Advantages and disadvantages of Central Bank Digital Currency:

Advantages:

1. Central bank digital currency furnishes more transactions efficient way than cash, making payments cheaper and quicker.
2. Central bank digital currency can be serviced as a backdrop to private sector-managed payment systems, avoiding a breakdown of the payment infrastructure during a crisis of confidence.
3. Central bank digital currency helps increase financial inclusion, providing low-income householders and those in sparsely populated areas easy access to digital payments and other financial products and services.
4. Central bank digital currency has the potential to ease the zero lower bound constraint on monetary policy.
5. Central bank digital currency brings informal economic activity out of the shadow, thereby broadening the tax base and reducing tax evasion, which adds up to higher tax revenue for the government.

Disadvantages:

1. Central bank digital currency has risk in digital or web-based as it is inclined to technological vulnerabilities, for example, hacking.
2. Central bank digital currency could, depending upon its structure, put the government in direct competition with the private sector in the provision of payment and financial services.
3. Central bank digital currency could end up precipitating the very risk—financial instability.

Countries in the world with CENTRAL BANK DIGITAL CURRENCIES [CBDC]:

1. The Bahamas [Sand Dollar]
2. China [e-CNY]
3. Nigeria [e-Naira]
4. Jamaica [JamDex]
5. India [Digital Rupee]
6. Russia [Digital Ruble]
7. Antigua & Barbuda
8. Dominica
9. Grenada
10. Montserrat
11. St. Kitts and Nevis
12. Saint Lucia
13. St. Vincent and The Grenadines [DCash]
14. Sweden
15. Ukraine
16. The United States of America
17. Tunisia
18. Venezuela
19. Marshall Islands
20. Senegal
21. United Arab Emirates
22. Ghana
23. Malaysia
24. Singapore
25. Thailand

The future of CBDC is growing enormously reaching over $250 billion within five years from now. It could change the monetary system. However, there are some potential risks associated with CBDCs. For instance, if citizens pull too much money out of banks at once and purchase CBDCs, it could trigger a run on banks. CBDCs through the government could also increase data privacy concerns. Also, some current legal frameworks are not comprehensive enough /

modernized enough to deal with the new forms of money. In the absence of robust legal systems, the issuance of CBDC poses legal, financial, and reputational risks for central banks.

CHAPTER 14

Feedback from Cryptocurrency Market Research Survey

Q1. Do you own and or cryptocurrencies?
A1. 86% said Yes; 14% said No.
Q2. When was the first time you bought cryptocurrency?
A2. $1% said one year ago; 2.0% said five years ago.
Q3. Could you tell me the reason to buy cryptocurrency?
A3. 60% said to invest in; 30% said to trade.
Q4. Do you purchase cryptocurrencies regularly?
A4. 60% said Yes; 40% said No.
Q5. What coins do you own?
A5. 45% said Bitcoin; 15% said Ethereum; 40% said other coins.

GLOSSARY

Algorithm: An Algorithm is a set of rules to follow to solve a problem or conduct a task.

Altcoin: Any cryptocurrency that is an alternative to Bitcoin.

Application Specific-Integrated Circuit [ASIC]: Refers to specialized computers that are made to do a very specific task [calculate hashes for Bitcoin's Proof-of-Work].

Bitcoin: The first decentralized cryptocurrency was released in 2009.

Block: A set of cryptocurrency transactions that have taken place and been verified within a certain amount of time.

Blockchain: A type of decentralized public digital ledger that contains blocks/records/transactions and forms the basis for how many cryptocurrencies work, using cryptography to link together blocks/records/transactions in a chain so that each block/record/transaction is linked with the previous one chronologically, preventing any tampering or revisionist history from occurring since it would be recognized immediately by other users on the network.

Central Bank Digital Currency [CBDC]: It is a digital fiat currency issued by the central bank, contrary to the cryptocurrency issued by a non-legislative party.

Centralized: A system of power where a central authority has control over the execution of operations. Often associated with a dictator style of rules and a single point of attack.

Cold Wallet: Wallets that are offline and require physical access to certain devices [hardware wallet, paper wallets]

Cryptocurrency: A form of digital asset that uses cryptography as its main security measure to control the creation of additional units and verify transactions on its decentralized network.

Cryptocurrency Wallet: An app or device where one's cryptocurrency transactions are stored. Cryptocurrency wallets allow users to send and receive cryptocurrency, by providing an Internet address to which tokens can be sent.

Cryptography: The use of cryptographic protocols or mathematical techniques to encrypt messages sent between parties which are then decrypted using a key for security purposes.

Decentralized: When something does not have any central control but rather operates independently through peer-to-peer networks and consensus algorithms instead, transactions cannot be reversed once confirmed on blockchains that do not have any central authority or place of residence since they are decentralized.

Decentralized applications (DApps): Decentralized applications are essentially software programs built and hosted on blockchain technology, providing users with various functions through peer-to-peer action rather than depending upon traditional intermediaries such as government or banks. Decentralized applications are frequently used to execute decentralized finance (DeFi) operations.

Decentralized Autonomous Organization (DAO): A cryptocurrency or business that is run by 'smart contracts' and governed by its token-holding community.

Decentralized Exchange (DEX): A system that allows for the trustless, peer-to-peer trading of cryptocurrencies without a third party or intermediary trading fees along the way.

Decentralized Finance (DeFi): It pushed the development of alternative decentralized blockchain-based financial applications without third parties. Decentralized finance applications include lending platforms, exchanges, prediction markets, and many more solutions built on top of various protocols such as Ethereum or Bitcoin.

Distributed Digital Ledger (DLT): A type of database that is spread out across several nodes in different locations and countries so that it can remain decentralized as well as transparent to those involved with keeping records on it. Every single node will hold a complete copy which is updated regularly through consensus algorithms when new transactions take place. This allows for faster processing speeds since multiple copies are already available rather than one central authority who has to distribute them from scratch if something does go wrong.

Ethereum: Ethereum is like Bitcoin in that it offers digital cash freed from the interference of governments, banks, and credit cards. It furnishes blockchain infrastructure that does more than just allow people to make transactions with cryptocurrency. There are a number of Ethereum-based applications available. They include smart contracts which are written in code and execute themselves. Some of the contracts support decentralized finance (DeFi), a process that eliminates the need for brokerages and other third parties in financial transactions. Ethereum supports NFTs [Non-fungible Token], which represent the ownership of something, either real or digital. The platform supports the development of other currencies.

Ethereum Virtual Machine (EVM): It helps to run *smart contracts* on Ethereum's blockchain by keeping track of their state and allowing them to be executed simultaneously across their network through consensus.

Exchange: Platforms that allow users to buy, sell, or trade cryptocurrencies for other digital currencies or traditional currencies such as the US dollar or euros.

Fiat Currency: A legal tender declared by the government. This can be backed by its economy and has an institution that regulates it (central bank). For example, British Pound (GBP) & US Dollar (USD).

Hash: A specific algorithm that maps data of any size to a fixed-size output.

Hot Wallet / Hot Storage: Any method of storing private keys for cryptocurrency that is connected to the Internet, such as a digital wallet offered by an app.

Initial Coin Offering [ICO]: If anyone or a group wants to launch a new cryptocurrency, they need funds to develop their software, or they just want to turbocharge trading in the new coin.

Ledger: A record of financial transactions that cannot be changed, only appended with new transactions.

Meme coin: A digital currency that doesn't have any inherent value and is used for social media purposes.

Mining: The process of creating new cryptocurrency units by solving complex mathematical problems, which are then verified and added to the blockchain. Mining is a decentralized mathematically intensive computational process by which cryptocurrency tokens are created and the blockchain ledger is maintained and secured.

Non-fungible Tokens (NFT): Digital assets that are unique and can't be replaced by generic items like coins. It is a unique cryptographic token generally used as a way to verify ownership of an intangible asset, such as a digital file, through blockchain technology.

Node: A connected computer that is part of a network, Blockchain in this case. All nodes are equal, and each one can be used to broadcast messages across the entire system. A computer or other device that helps maintain a cryptocurrency's blockchain by participating in the transaction-verification process. Each individual device used by a miner is a single node.

Open-Source: Software is a type of software released under a license in which the copyright holder grants users the right to study, change, and distribute the software to anyone and for any purpose.

Peer-to-peer: A system where two parties can conduct financial transactions with each other without involving a third party, like a bank. The blockchain is an example of this since it connects nodes in its network directly to one another and allows them to share data/transactions freely between themselves.

Public key: Similar to a username, it's a shareable string of numbers and letters that allows users to send and receive cryptocurrency.

A cryptographic key that allows a user to receive cryptocurrency from another user but cannot be used to send funds. It usually consists of sixty-four characters to encrypt your wallet or make digital signatures.

Private key: Similar to a password, a private number that allows an owner access to their cryptocurrency. A cryptographic key that allows users to send cryptocurrency from their wallet but cannot be used to receive funds. It usually consists of 64 characters which you use for decrypting your wallet or making digital signatures.

Proof-of-Authority [POA]: A consensus algorithm that assigns block validation queues based on identity and reputation.

Proof-of-Stake [POS]: A consensus algorithm that assigns a block validation queue based on the coins/tokens locked in by the validation.

Proof-of-Work [POW]: A consensus algorithm in which a block is validated via mathematical hashing.

Signature: The method by which the owner of a private key proves that they approved a transaction with cryptocurrency.

Smart contract: A piece of code that is executed on the blockchain after certain conditions have been met. This allows developers to create decentralized applications without having to build their blockchains from scratch.

Stablecoin: A cryptocurrency designed to minimize price volatility, usually by pegging its value or supply against a physical asset such as fiat currencies like US Dollar.

Token: Token is a digital representation of an asset or utility that resides on a blockchain network. It can be created, transferred and owned by participants within the network. A unit value used for various purposes within a crypto ecosystem. Tokens can represent any cryptocurrencies.

Tokenization: It works by creating a digital token that represents an asset, such as currency. This token is then stored on a blockchain, which is a decentralized digital ledger that can be used to store and transfer data in a secure transparent way.

Transactional fee: The sum of money paid to miners to confirm transactions into blocks and add them to the blockchain network.

Wallet: A digital location used to store crypto funds by storing private and public keys that provide access to your cryptocurrency holdings.

BIBLIOGRAPHY/REFERENCES

Agur, Itai, Anil Ari, and Giovanni Dell'ariccia. 2021. "Designing Central Bank Digital Currencies." *Journal of Monetary Economics.*

Andolfatto, David. 2021. "Assessing the Impact of Central Bank Digital Currency on Central Banks." *Economic Journal 131*, no. 634: 525–540.

Arvidsson, Nikolas. 2019. *Building a Cashless Society: Swedish Route to the Future of Cash Payments. SpringerBriefs in Economics.* Cham, Switzerland: Springer Nature.

Aslanidis, Nektarios, Aurelio F. Bariviera, and Oscar Martinez-Ibañez. 2019. "An Analysis of Cryptocurrencies Conditions Cross Correlations." *Finance Research Letters 31*, 130–137.

Auer, Raphael, and Rainer Boehme. 2020. "The Technology of Retail Central Bank Digital Currency." *BIS Quarterly Review* (March): 85–100.

Bank of Canada, European Central Bank, Bank of Japan, Sveriges Riksbank, Swiss National Bank, Bank of England, Board of Governors of the Federal Reserve, and Bank of International Settlements. 2020. "Central Bank Digital Currencies: Foundational Principles and Core Features." *Bank for International Settlements*. https://www.bis.org/pub/othp33.pdf.

Bank of England. 2020. "Central Bank Digital Currency Opportunities, Challenges and Design." *Bank of England*. https://www.bankofengland.co.uk/-/media/boe/files/paper/2020/central-bank-digital-currency-opportunities-challenges-and-design.pdf.

Bano, Shehar, Alberto Sonnino, Mustafa Al-Bassam, Sarah Azouvi, Patrick McCorry, Sarah Meilkejohn, and George Danezis. 2019. *SoK: Consensus in the Age of Blockchains.*

Barrdear, John, and Michael Kumhof. 2016. "The Microeconomics of Central Bank-Issued Digital Currencies." *Bank of England.*

Bech, Morten Linneman, and Rodney Garratt. 2017. "Central Bank Cryptocurrencies." *Bank for International Settlement Quarterly Review.* pp. 55–70.

Bergara, Mario, and Jorge Ponce. 2018. *Central Bank Digital Currency: The Uruguayan e-Peso Case.* Unpublished manuscript, Central Bank of Uruguay, Montevideo.

Bonneau, Joseph, Andrew Miller, Jeremy Clark, Arvind Narayanan, Joshua Kroll, and Edward W. Felten. 2015. *Research Perspectives and Challenges for Bitcoin and Cryptocurrencies.*

Bordo, Michael D., and Andrew T. Levin. 2017. *Central Bank Digital Currency and the Future of Monetary Policy.*

Brainard, Lael. 2018. *Cryptocurrencies, Digital Currencies, and Distributed Ledger Technologies: What Are We Learning?*

Brunnermeier, Markus K., Harold James, and Jean-Pierre Landau. 2019. *The Digitalization of Money.*

Camara, Noelia, Enestor Dos Santos, Francisco Grippa, Javier Sebastian, Fernando Soto, and Cristina Varela. 2018. *Central Bank Digital Currencies: An Assessment of Their Adoption in Latin America.*

Carstens, Agustin. 2018. *Money in the Digital Age: What Role for Central Banks?*

Casey, Michael, and Joshua S. Gans. 2019. *Initial Coin Offerings and the Value of Crypto Tokens.*

Chen, Kaiji, Jue Ren, and Tao Zha. 2018. "The Nexus of Monetary Policy and Shadow Banking in China." *American Economic Review 108,* no. 12: pp. 3891–3936.

Clark, John, Nathan Converse, Brahima Coulibaly, and Steven Kamin. 2019. "Emerging Market Capital Flows and U.S. Monetary Policy." *International Finance 23,* no.1 pp. 2–17.

Coeure, Benoit. 2019. *Digital Challenges to the International Monetary and Financial System.*

Collomb, Alexis, Primavera De Filippi, and Klara Sok. 2019. "Blockchain Technology and Financial Regulation: A Risk-Based Approach to the Regulation of ICOs." *European Journal of Risk Regulation 10*, no. 2: pp. 263–314.

Cong, Lin William, and Zhiguo He. 2019. "Blockchain Disruption and Smart Contracts." *Review of Financial Studies 32*, no. 5: pp. 1754–1797.

Conti, Mauro, Sandeep Kumar E., Chhagan Lal, and Sushmita Ruj. 2017. *A Survey on Security and Privacy Issues of Bitcoin*. Institute of Electrical and Electronic Engineers.

Corbae, Dean, and Pablo D'Erasmo. 2020. "Rising Bank Concentration." *Journal of Economic Dynamic and Control.*

Dain, Philip, Steven Goldfeder, Tyler Kell, Yungxi Li, Xueyuan Zhao, Iddo Bentov, Laurence Breidenbach, and Ari Jules. 2019. *Front running, Transacting Reordering, and Consensus Instability in Decentralized Exchanges.*

Danezis, George, and Sarah Meiklejohn. 2016. *Central Banked Cryptocurrencies.*

Demirguc-Kunt, Asli, Leora Klapper, Dorothy Singer, Saniya Ansar, and Jake Hess. 2018. *Global Findex Database 2017: Measuring Financial Inclusion and the Fintech Revolution.*

Dhawan, Anirudh, and Talis J. Putnins. 2020. *A New Wolf in Town Pump and Dump Manipulation in Cryptocurrency Markets.*

Easley, David, Maureen O'Hara, and Soumya Basu. 2019. "From Mining to Markets: The Evolution of Bitcoin Transaction Fees." *Journal of Financial Economics 134*, pp. 91–109.

Engert, Walter, and Ben S. C. Fung. 2017. "*Central Bank Digital Currency: Motivations and Implications.*"

Fernandez-Villaverde, Jesus, Daniel Sanches, Linda Schilling, and Harald Uhlig. 2020. *Central Bank Digital Currency.*

Foley, Sean, Jonathan R. Karlsen, and Talis J. Putnins. 2019. "Sex, Drugs, and Bitcoin: How Much Illegal Activity is Financed through Cryptocurrencies." *Review of Financial Studies 32*, no. 5: pp. 1798–1853.

Fung, Be S.C., and Hanna Halaburda. 2016. *Central Bank Digital Currencies: A Framework for Assessing Why and How.*

Garratt, Rodney, and Neil Wallace. 2018. "Bitcoin 1, Bitcoin2,...: An Experiment in Privately Issued Outside Monies." *Economic Inquiry 56*, no. 3: pp. 1887–1897.

Goldberg, Linda S. 2010. *Is the International Role of the Dollar Changing*? Economics and Finance.

Goldstein, Itay, Wei Jiang, and G. Andrew Karolyi. 2019. "To FinTech and Beyond." *Review of Financial Studies 32*, no. 5: pp. 1647–1661.

Griffin, John M., and Amin Shams. 2020. "Is Bitcoin Really Un-tethered?" *Journal of Finance 75*, no. 4: pp. 1775–2321.

Grimmelmann, James. 2019. "All Smart Contracts Are Ambiguous." *Journal of Law and Innovation 2*, no. 1: pp. 1–22.

Grym, Aleksi. 2020. "Lessons Learned from the World's First CBDC." *Bank of Finland Economics Review*, no. 8: pp. 1–22.

Howell, Sabrina, Marina Niessner, and David Yermack. 2021. "Initial Coin Offerings: Financing Growth with Cryptocurrency Sales." *Review of Financial Studies.*

Ingves, Stefan. 2017. *Do We Need an e-Krona?*

Ismail, Leila, and Huned Materwala. 2019. "A review of Blockchain Architecture and Consensus Protocols: Use Cases, Challenges, and Solutions." *Symmetry 11*, no. 10: 1198.

Ju, Lan, Timothy Lu, and Zhiyong Tu. 2016. "Capital Flight and Bitcoin Regulation." *International Review of Finance 16*, no. 3: pp. 445–455.

Mancini-Griffoli, Tommaso, Maria Soledad Martinez Peria, Itai Agur, John Kiff, Adina Popescu, and Celine Rochon. 2018. *Casting Light on Central Bank Digital Currency.*

Massad, Timothy. 2019. *It's time to Strengthen the Regulation of Crypto-Assets.*

Mora, Camilo, Randi L. Rollins, Katie Taladay, Micheal B. Kantar, Mason K. Chock, Niuo Shimada, and Erik C. Franklin. 2018. "Bitcoin Emissions Alone Could Push Global Warming above 2 degrees Centigrade." *Nature Climate Change 8*, no. 11: pp. 931–933.

Narayanan, Arvind, Joseph Bonneau, Edward Felten, Andrew Miller, and Steven Goldfeder. 2016. *Bitcoin and Cryptocurrency Tech-*

nologies: A Comprehensive Introduction. Princeton, NJ: Princeton University Press.

Qiu, Tanh, Ruidong Zhang, and Yuan Gao. 2019. *Ripple versus SWIFT: Transforming Cross Border Remittance Using Blockchain Technology*

Raskin, Max, and David Yermack. 2018. *Digital Currencies, Decentralized Ledgers, and the Future of Central Banking.*

Schilling, Linda, and Harald Uhlig, 2018. *Some Simple Bitcoin Economics.*

Schneider, John. 2017. *FinTech and Financial Innovation: Drivers and Depth.*

Stoll, Christian, Lena Klaasen, and Ulrich Gallersdorfer. 2019. "The Carbon Footprint of Bitcoin." *Joule 3*, no. 7: pp. 1647–1661.

Vigna, Paul, and Michael Casey. 2016. *The Age of Cryptocurrency: How Bitcoin and Blockchain Are Changing the World Economic Order*. New York: Picador.

Yao, Qian. 2017. "The Application of Digital Currency in Interbank Cash Transfer Scenario." *Finance Computerizing 5*: pp. 16–19.

ABOUT THE AUTHOR

Dan Vivek Nathan holds double master's degrees, an MBA, as well as an MSc, and a professional postgraduate diploma in marketing management from institutions in the UK. He has written four books: *Cryptocurrency Empowers Global Financial Systems* [Archway Publishers/Simon Schuster—2023], *Entrepreneurship Education Enriches Entrepreneurial Management in Digital Age* [Newman Springs Publishing—2022], *Global Market/Marketing Research in 21st Century and Beyond* [Newman Springs Publishing—2022], and *Know-How of Branding Products And Services in the Digital Space* [Newman Springs Publishing—2022].

www.ingramcontent.com/pod-product-compliance
Lightning Source LLC
LaVergne TN
LVHW090413210926
848480LV00002B/554
9798896171072